Plain Talks

Plain Talks on Marriage

Rev. Fulgence Meyer, OFM

TAN Books
Gastonia, North Carolina

Nihil Obstat:
Fr. Valentinus Schaaf, O.F.M.,
Censor Deputatus

Imprimi Potest:
Fr. Edmund Klein, O.F.M.,
Provincial Minister

Imprimatur:
Joannes T. McNicholas,
Archbishop of Cincinnati
February 2, 1927

Originally published in 1927 by Franciscan Fathers of the Province of St. John the Baptist Cincinnati, Ohio.

Editor's Note: a few sentences and footnotes were added to elaborate on the author's words. Revisions and deletions have been included to make the work more accessible to the modern reader's sensitivities.

Cover design by Chris Pelicano

ISBN: 978-1-5051-2110-0
Kindle ISBN: 978-1-5051-2111-7
ePUB ISBN: 978-1-5051-2112-4

Published in the United States by
TAN Books
PO Box 269
Gastonia, NC 28053
www.TANBooks.com

Printed in the United States of America

To all the noble Christian husbands and wives—who, by their mutual love and holiness of life, aim to make their conjugal union a true copy of the union of Christ and His Church, this book is heartily and appreciatively dedicated by The Author.

Contents

Publisher's Preface

"The cross is the bed of my spouses; it's there that I have them taste the delights of my love,"[1] said Our Lord to St. Margaret Mary. In the Douay-Rheims translation of St. John's Passion narrative, Christ's final recorded words from the Cross were, *Consummatum Est*, "It is consummated" (Jn 19:30). No other bible translation uses these words—words which illuminate the marital act. On the Cross, Our Lord gave everything to His spouse, the Church, pouring out every drop of blood so that she might be holy and blameless like her Bridegroom (see Col. 1:22). From the pulpit of Mount Calvary, Our Lord gave all couples the greatest marriage preparation course ever. This course does not end after a couple exchanges their vows; rather, it begins. A sacramental marriage becomes valid not when a husband and wife say I do but when they consummate their love by giving themselves to each

1 Therese of Lisieux, *St. Therese of Lisieux, Her Last Conversations* (Washington D.C.: ICS Publications, 1977), 136.

other freely, totally, faithfully, and fruitfully in the marital act. Hence, St. Paul was not using a loose analogy when he said, "Husbands, love your wives, as Christ also loved the church, and delivered himself up for it: That he might sanctify it, cleansing it by the washing of water in the word of life" (Eph. 5:25–26). No, St. Paul was giving us a vibrant and robust metaphor. Be crucified, husband. Be crucified to selfishness. Be crucified to sin, especially sexual sins. Do not take up your cross only once, but each day of your life. If you are crucified with Christ, then you and your spouse, with God's grace, will live happily ever after in Eternity.

As Our Lord's piercing words to St. Margaret Mary reveal, marriage is the cross and not a bed of roses. The honeymoon will not last forever; temptations and trials will come. And yet, just as suffering endears mankind to the heavenly Spouse, so too will suffering unite you to your earthly spouse. It is when you reject the cross and seek your own pleasure that you set yourself up for divorce. Make no mistake, the marital bed has been tainted by our perverted culture and defiled by sin. Instead of having one bride until death, a married man can now have thousands of brides, albeit fantasy ones. Instead of seeing his wife unveiled for the first time on his wedding night, many young men today have seen countless unveiled women virtually or in reality. Today, more and more women are also struggling with pornography. Perhaps this wound was inherited from their own parents whose lack of purity infects future generations. Yes, there is such a thing as generational sins; vice is readily passed onto one's children.

When the late Fr. Fulgence Meyer, OFM, wrote this book in the 1920s to counsel married couples on sexual morality and forming a truly Catholic home, he never could have imagined how the cancer of pornography would creep into the Church. Pornography is the most confessed sin by men. Yes, pornography is the greatest threat to the sacrament of marriage. But there is hope. Hope in the power of the sacraments, especially confession. But do not wait until you are married to convert your heart. The wedding ring will not take away your lust. You must choose your spouse now. While Our Lord's public ministry began around the age of thirty with His Baptism in the Jordan, Jesus prepared Himself from the womb. The same is true for you. Since your childhood, you have been preparing for your vocation. Who you are today is largely the result of your parents, how they disciplined you, the values they instilled in you, and the habits you acquired. Now, along with your spouse, you have been entrusted with the responsibility to prepare your children for their future vocations.

Although the sacrament of marriage is daunting at times, the saints are always there to supply timely help. Call upon Our Lady, Mother Most Pure, and her most chaste spouse, St. Joseph, to give you a clean heart. Be the holy spouse that your wife or husband need you to be today. Be the holy parents your children need you to be today. Remember, Christ Crucified is the only solid foundation for a lasting marriage.

Dear Husband, each morning you spend a few minutes before a mirror combing your hair, or perhaps shaving your beard. But do you each morning spend some time quietly looking at the true mirror, the holy crucifix? When you see Our Lord's body, drenched in blood and scars, does it not reveal to you who you are and who you ought to become? There is no greater examination of conscience than gazing on Him, Who willingly stripped Himself of everything so that you might no longer glory in the flesh. The holy crucifix, my brothers, is what total self-donation and humility looks like—to be poured out completely, to be crushed like grapes in the wine press of love, and to hold nothing back from one's spouse. To see the cross of your vocation but to choose it anyway is authentic, sacrificial love. It is the path to glory. Pride, selfishness, and lust have no place in the heart of a true lover of the Cross.

Dear Wife, each morning you spend time before the mirror so that you might look more beautiful for yourself, your spouse, your friends, even total strangers. But do you also spend time before some image or statue of Our Lady, she who perfectly mirrored her Son's virtues of love, humility, poverty, and obedience? Our Lady is the mirror of humility, true femininity, and receptivity. Seek her intercession and she will teach you how to give yourself more fully to your husband. She will teach you generosity, but most of all, she will slowly plant her virtuous flowers in the garden of your heart—where a living Mary garden will flourish. A wife who seeks to forget herself as Mary did, who seeks to serve her husband, will find him more eager to sacrifice for her.

The marital wisdom presented in this little work, in these honest and open plain talks, is timeless, tried, and true. Dear Catholic Parent, we are on a great stage and Our Lord, the saints, and the angels are watching us. Let us not miss the opportunity to love our spouse as Christ loved His Church. Let us not miss the opportunity to raise our children to become great saints so that we might praise God with them now and for all eternity.

—The Publisher

Preface to the Original Edition

This treatise is an elaboration of the conference which the author addresses to married men and women in missions. He is publishing it in the interest of people who are married, or who are about to be married: and who are bent on making their marriage what God intends it should be: a source of happiness and a nursery of holiness.

Fr. Fulgence Meyer, OFM

Chapter I

Happiness in Marriage

"Blessed are all they that fear the Lord; that walk in His ways. . . . Thy wife as a fruitful vine, on the sides of thy house. Thy children as olive plants, round about thy table. And mayst thou see thy children's children. . . . Peace upon Israel" (Ps. 127).

In Rome, several years ago, one of the Reverend Consultors of the Sacred Congregation of the Sacraments told the writer, that the sacrament of matrimony gives the congregation more work and trouble than all the other sacraments taken together. Every bishop, pastor, missionary and confessor has about the same story to tell when he measures not so much the volume of the work as the worry it gives him. Nor will this surprise us when we consider that the sacrament of matrimony affects human nature in its most sensitive and self-assertive domain. It intends to moderate and regulate love, than which there is no more personal element, and no greater force in man or woman.

A Delicate, Yet Grateful Task

It is not without a degree of considerable diffidence and hesitancy, if not of positive reluctance, that a Catholic priest sets about to discuss the sacred and intimate relations of husband and wife. This is a most difficult and trying task because of the very important and highly delicate subjects that have to be treated, and which are altogether foreign to a priest's personal life and consecration. He fears lest he may say a word or use a phrase inadvisedly, and thus create a false or sinister impression; or he may unwittingly omit to mention one or the other point that deserve to be emphasized; or, in general, his very knowledge of, and references to, certain phases of married life may be misconstrued.

On the other hand no treatise produces richer, deeper and more far-reaching results than the prudent and sympathetic discussion of the vocational duties of married men and women. It bears fruit not only with reference to those who read it, but also to countless others who will be indirectly benefited by it, and who, in times to come, may even owe their very existence to it.

The Pillar and the Cloud

Moreover, in offering enlightenment and inspiration to good Catholic fathers and mothers, the Catholic priest is satisfied, that he has an opportunity of paying off a part of the great debt he owes Almighty God for the signal favor the Lord bestowed upon him in giving him good Catholic parents, which is known to be one of the greatest graces which heaven dispenses. No matter how many years he lives or whatever career path he chooses, it always remains one of his sweetest thrills and most solid joys, when he can look back upon his youth and childhood, and say: "My parents were true Christians, in thought, word and deed. They were the outstanding grace of God for me in my life. They were parents after God's own heart, and lovers to the core of Christ and His Church. Never did I hear them say, or see them do anything, that was unbecoming their dignity and profession as Catholic parents. Their example was an eloquent and a continuous sermon on the beauty of virtue and the value of religion to their children, clearly pointing out to them, and rendering easy for them, the way to heaven, the promised land, even as a pillar of fire by night, and as a sheltering cloud by day. May the Lord be eternally praised and thanked for the priceless gift of so good a father and so dear a mother."

As Others See Us

The married couples who read this book are trying their best, I have reason to believe, to become true Christian parents. It will be my object, in this essay, to hearten and help them to keep on endeavoring to live up to the ideal of Catholic husbands and wives, and, respectively, of Catholic fathers and mothers. I do not intend to scold, or find fault, or embarrass anyone: but I aim to instruct, comfort and encourage. We all need to be periodically enlightened and animated regarding our particular life duties. The Holy Father, the cardinals, bishops, priests, friars, brothers, and nuns make a retreat or a mission once a year. They are then told very plainly what their duties are within their state of life; they are warned against certain dangers; and their defects and shortcomings are pointed out to them, without gloss or varnish. They appreciate this much, and are sincerely grateful for it, conscious as they are of the blinding influence of self-love, and of the advantage there is in seeing ourselves as others see us. For the same reason I feel that my married readers are going to welcome this instruction.

On the Stage of Life

Life is often compared to a stage, upon which we are all given a part to play. God Himself has assigned our individual roles to us. In calling you to the married state, He has allotted to you a distinguished and arduous part on the stage of life. And if you are a parent, your part is immensely more sublime and difficult. It is no small task to be a Catholic husband, wife, and parent. This requires virtue and ability of the highest order. Whoever in a dramatic play must represent a difficult character, is glad to have someone instruct him and provide him with helpful cautions, hints and suggestions. I shall now attempt to do this in your behalf regarding the conduct of your married life.

God Has Chosen You

You must above all remember that God has chosen you for the part you must play on the stage of life; and since He has chosen you for it, He will supply you with the strength you need to conduct yourself with virtue. Even if you married frivolously and thoughtlessly, or through mere passion or spite: now that you are bound by your vows, you can be sure that God intended you should be bound thus: and consequently you can count on His help to achieve happiness and holiness in the marriage you have legitimately contracted, and from which you can no longer withdraw. All regrets as to what else might have been, had you not married, are idle and futile. What matters now is that you make the most of your present situation through good sense and the grace of God. Do not make things worse by dwelling gloomily and pessimistically on your real or imaginary mistake in marrying as you did, and by thus increasing the evil effects of it: but rather make a virtue out of necessity, and turn your mistake, whatever it was, into a stepping stone to sanctity and everlasting glory. To those who entered the convent or the priesthood without a vocation from on high, and who realized their mistake after they had bound themselves by the holy vows for life, St. Augustine said: "If you are not called, see to it that you be called." Similarly married people who, after they are married a while, find that they made a mistake in marrying at all, will apply the best remedy to their hard situation not by unavailing complaints or morbid self-pity, but by doing what they can to render their actual married life their real vocation. With the aid of God's grace many have done this to their great contentment and sanctification. What others have done, you can do too, with the assistance of the same grace. Spiritually and religiously you may even thrive better for being unfortunately married. You must live your vows to the fullest and not look back on whether you should have been a priest, religious, single, or even married to someone else. Be holy now. The path to sanctity is the vocation God calls you to, not necessarily the higher calling, or even the one you imagine to be better.

A Vale of Tears

The fact alone that you are not fully happy in your married life, is not by any means a sign that you were not called or destined for it. No one, in the married or any other state of life, is completely happy on this earth. God did not intend that anyone should be entirely happy. This earth will always be a vale of tears no matter how we arrange it, in marriage, in the single life in the world, in the cloister, in the priesthood, and everywhere else. Do not think you can escape the cross, for the cross will follow you. If you do not embrace it, it will crush you. Remember, the cross is only temporary. We are merely pilgrims or tourists steering towards our eternal home, and the more we are disposed to put up with the discomforts and annoyances of tourists or travelers, the less chagrined shall we be. Even in paradise there was the forbidden tree and the insidious serpent. No home or family life can therefore be expected to be without some trouble and worry. All we can do is to achieve a relative happiness here below, as a preparation for an eternal happiness beyond. Marriage offers a good opportunity for the accomplishment of both.

An Infallible Recipe

What, then, is the recipe of happiness for a married person? It is contained in the words of my text: "Blessed are all they that fear the Lord." This is the recipe given by God Himself. If anyone knows the way to true and lasting happiness, it is the Lord Who created our heart and gave it its vehement and incessant craving for happiness. He condenses the whole manner of achieving happiness in the words I have quoted. All other recipes of happiness, divergent from this one, no matter by whom they have been or are given, are false and misleading. There is but one way for a Catholic couple to become thoroughly and permanently happy, and that one way is the fear of the Lord.

How does a Catholic couple practice and manifest the fear of the Lord? First by worshiping God faithfully. They say their prayers every morning and evening. In their home, which is duly blessed, they pray aloud with the family before and after meals; this, too, when guests are present, let them be Catholics or not. Grace at table always makes a good impression on company worth having.

Family Prayer

Outside of their personal prayers, which should include the daily examination of conscience and an act of perfect contrition, Catholic parents will see to it, that the family recite a certain prayer in common, called family prayer. Not only is each individual member of the family expected to pray, but the family as such should in concert worship God and consecrate itself to Him afresh every day. Father and mother and all the children kneel before the family crucifix and recite together the rosary, or a litany, or some other prayers as a homage of the family towards the Lord. The best time to perform this prayer will usually be immediately after supper before the family disbands or retires. The prayer need not be long—it should not be so long as to weary and bore the children—but it should be said regularly and constantly by the entire family.

Nothing is more apt to keep the spirit of God and of faith in a family, and to assure it of the Lord's continual blessing and protection than this family prayer. And nothing will be more likely to guarantee the perseverance of all the family members in the true Church than this family prayer. Your children will not remain with you long. Soon they will disperse into various directions. They will be assailed by all kinds of temptations against virtue and religion, and they may for a time grow lukewarm and careless in the practice of their holy faith. But if in their childhood and youth they were held to take part in the daily family prayer, the remembrance of it, when with father and mother and brothers and sisters they dedicated themselves to God anew from day to day, will haunt them persistently, and give them no rest until they return to the faith of their fathers and its regular and conscientious practice. If, therefore, you have not yet introduced family prayer into your home, do it at once. St. Augustine says that every Christian home is a little parish for itself. The parents are the priests, and the children are the members of the parish. It behooves priests to guide their parishes particularly in prayer; parents have the same office in their homes; and wherever it is well done, it invariably proves to be their most grateful and productive office. The best time to start this family prayer is at the very beginning of married life.

The Precious Crucifix

The family crucifix should be the most precious object and should form the most cherished and frequented shrine of the entire house. Around it centers the sweetest and dearest family memories and traditions. Perhaps it is an heirloom that has come down from father to son, or from mother to daughter in uncounted generations; or perhaps it is a wedding present from the priest or some dear friend. When the young couple for the first time entered their own household, it was before this crucifix that they mutually renewed the pledge of their great love and lasting union. And when the first trials of married life came upon them, it was before this crucifix that they poured out their grief together and asked for solace, courage, and strength. When God gave them the grand blessing of their first child, they again knelt before this crucifix in warm appreciation and fervent gratitude. They repeated this act of whole-hearted joy and recognition at each new addition to the family circle. When God, in His inscrutable providence, withdrew one of the children He had given, perhaps the best and dearest, or the only one, their first impulse was to throw themselves down before this sacred crucifix, and exclaim grief-stricken but resigned: "The Lord gave, and the Lord hath taken away: as it has pleased the Lord, so is it done: blessed be the Name of the Lord" (Job 1:21). And at the death of each member of the family this hallowed crucifix receives the last conscious sigh and kiss of love from him or her who derived their sweetest solace from it in all the circumstances and fortunes of life.

A Catholic couple will give evidence of their fear of the Lord by closely keeping the commandments of God and the Church. This observance must have become such a habit with them and be so ingrained in their character that their children are convinced their parents would rather die than willfully miss holy Mass on a Sunday or holy days of obligation or violate the Friday or other days of fast and abstinence, or otherwise transgress God's holy law. This conviction on the part of their sons and daughters will be the best Catholic education the parents can give them.

The Hunter and His Son

A man who had long given up the practice of his holy faith had a son of about fourteen years of age who had just received his first solemn Communion with sincere piety. The father was very fond of him. Shortly after the boy's first solemn Communion the father accosted him one Sunday morning, saying he should get ready, for they were to go out together to hunt all day. The boy replied: "Papa, I must go to Mass first." At this the father seemed to be peeved, and he rejoined: "Oh, you need not go to Mass now anymore; you are getting old enough to have more liberty." Now the boy appeared hurt, and asked: "Papa, does not the Third Commandment say: 'Remember that thou keep holy the Sabbath Day'?" "Third Commandment, nothing," answered the irate father; "that does not mean anything." The boy gravely looked up at his father and said solemnly: "Papa, if the Third Commandment does not mean anything, then the Fourth Commandment which says: 'Honor thy father and thy mother,' does not count either. If I do not have to honor God, I need not honor you." At this utterance, the father grew pensive. He feared if he would not relent, he would lose his hold on his son. He therefore said cautiously: "Well, maybe it is better that you go to Mass; and I will go with you." He continued to accompany his son to Mass ever after to his own and the family's welfare and happiness. The reason many Catholic parents lose out with their children and have no sway over them is often because they themselves disobey God and ignore His authority. "If God's authority means so little to them," the children argue, "why should my parents' authority mean anything to me?"

A Catholic couple shows the fear of the Lord by receiving the sacraments worthily and often. They appear at the Holy Altar every Sunday. They would dread to take the chance of doing without the heavenly food of our Lord's Body and Blood longer than that. They go more frequently, if possible; even every day. They not only approach the holy rail themselves, but they see to it, that all the members of the family are at least weekly communicants provided they are in a state of grace. Their example alone will usually be a sufficient factor to bring this about.

The Parish Church

A Catholic couple takes a lively and active interest in the parish church and its material and spiritual well-being. They know that the Catholic Church is represented to them by their parish church; hence whatever pride and goodwill they entertain for the true Church are centered first and foremost upon their parish church; for the best way to have the Church at large to thrive is to have each individual parish church to prosper. Their interest in their parish church must consist more in deeds and sacrifices than in words. They will be generous in their contributions to the church. They realize that the duty of supporting the church is as binding as the duty of Sunday Mass; and they fulfill the one as eagerly and conscientiously as the other. They never complain of being too heavily taxed for their church; they cheerfully give what their circumstances allow, and regret that they cannot give more. They are not only ready with large donations here and there, but they rather make their ordinary and regular contributions as high as they can reasonably make them; and they enjoy having them to be so high that they hurt, in the sense that they force them to deny themselves certain unnecessary pleasures or indulgences in their interest.

Holy Name Society

A Catholic couple belongs to the respective parish societies, knowing that in unity there is strength. The husband will be particularly glad and proud to belong to the Holy Name Society,[2] which stands for the ideals that are dearest to the heart of every good Catholic man; and he will never fail to be present at the general monthly Communion of the society, appreciating, as he does, the wonderful edification and stimulation there is in the sight of a body of men receiving our Lord together and professing their unstinted

2 The Holy Name Society was very popular at the time of this work. The Holy Name Society traces its roots to the thirteenth century with an emphasis on promoting devotion to the Holy Name.

and everlasting loyalty to Him in public before their wives and children and the entire parish. For the same reason, and with the same fervor the wife will be an active member of the Altar Society. And both will urge their children to affiliate themselves with the parish societies appropriate to their age and condition.

Picnics and Festivals

A good Catholic man not only contributes liberally towards his parish church, but he is also ready to render his personal services in its behalf. When he is asked to serve as an usher, or officer of one of the societies, or a member of a committee, or a member of the choir, he cheerfully accepts and performs his respective duties to the best of his ability, considering himself privileged the while to work for God and His sacred cause. Whenever the parish has certain events in the manner of picnics, card parties, socials, and the like, he and his wife show interest and active cooperation according to their circumstances, and they have the family to do the same. They will not be guilty of, nor will they tolerate that the members of their household be guilty of un-Catholic pride, conceit, and snobbery, that prompt aloofness from these ordinary and general parish gatherings and activities, as being beneath their station and dignity.

"E Pluribus Unum"[3]

Nothing makes so strongly for the material and spiritual welfare and progress of a parish as union and harmony of its members. Wherever there is a united front and a concerted action towards a given goal, success is bound to follow. The only way to achieve and hold this desired union and harmony is the recognition of the lawful and God-given authority on the part of the entire parish. The authority is represented by the pastor in charge. As he is finally responsible for the condition of the parish, all its members should yield to his guidance and government. If this is done, even though his plans or decisions may not be the wisest in themselves, there will nevertheless be good and substantial results. For after all, as has been well said, the best of governments is invariably that in which all the subjects heartily concur. While on the other hand there is no greater menace to the progress and life of a parish than dissensions, feuds, and factions among the members, or between the members and the head of the parish.

Active as they are for their home church, a good Catholic couple will not allow their interest to concentrate on it to such a degree as to be completely absorbed by it, so they fail to take notice of the Church at large and its diocesan, national and universal needs. This sentiment would

3 *E Pluribus Unum* is a Latin phrase that means "One from many."

smack distinctly of selfish localism or provincialism that are antagonistic to Catholicism, which embraces the entire world. A good Catholic couple will therefore take a lively interest also in the ecclesiastical affairs beyond their parish and contribute according to their capacity to the diocesan collections, as well as to those for the domestic and foreign missions, and most of all to that for the Holy Father in Rome.

A House of God

And again, since, as was said above, the parents are the priests of the little parish, which is their family and their home, they will at once take it upon themselves to give their home the air of a house of God. In other words, they will supply it with those emblems that ought to have a place in every Catholic home. Of these emblems the first and foremost is the crucifix of which mention was made above. Besides it there ought to be other representations of our Lord, His Mother, and the saints, placed about the home. While the house needs not to be turned into a holy picture gallery, yet a prudent selection of holy pictures will become a Catholic home well. They are indicative of faith, and of a certain gratitude for, and pride in, the faith. Meanwhile they are a continuous reminder of God and His saints, the heroes, and heroines of virtue, to the family, and thus provide it with a potent stimulant to piety and goodness.

Every Catholic home should have on hand two candlesticks and two blessed wax candles to be used in cases of sickness for the administration of the sacraments; also a bottle containing holy water.

The Holy Bible

A copy of the Holy Bible, of the Lives of the Saints, and of some good explanation of Catholic beliefs and practices should be found in every Catholic home. It should moreover keep at least one Catholic magazine together with the Catholic newspaper of the diocese or province.[4] The parents are not only to make this provision, but they are also to set the example in the regular and wholesome reading of these books and periodicals and cultivate a taste for them in themselves and their children, by often and prudently making their contents the subject of the family conversation. At the same time they will be careful to shut their home to all literature of a dangerous or dubious character, even as they will rigidly prohibit in it profane and other language that is unbecoming in the house of God, namely

---

4 Today there is a shift to Catholic websites and blogs, which can be spiritually fruitful.

the little temple over which they have the charge and the responsibility.

To God What Is God's: to Caesar What Is Caesar's

Good Catholics are not only loyal members of their Church, but also dutiful citizens of the state. Even as it is an inestimable privilege to belong to the true Church, so it is a great boon to be a citizen of the United States of America. Catholics show their appreciation of the latter favor by conscientiously paying their taxes and observing the laws of the country. Even though they may not be in sympathy with a certain law: as long as it is on the statute books they will observe it from motives of obedience to the civil authority, which they know is constituted and supported by God.[5] There are few countries in the world in which the Church is given so much liberty and room for her expansion, development and activity as in the United States; and for this reason we Catholics ought to be particularly devoted to the maintenance of our country's laws and institutions.

Catholics will do their duty as to this especially by contributing their share to procure a good and wise government.

---

5 Note: laws which violate one's conscience and are contrary to the Catholic Church's teachings should not be observed. See the *Catechism of the Church* for more details.

They will take a judicious interest in the political situation by voting wisely and efficiently. They will vote at every federal, state, and important local election. All things being equal, they will support their fellow-Catholics in their campaigns for public offices[6] to insure a just proportion of their co-religionists among the civil officials of the land.

The Mighty Ballot

While our Church enjoys great freedom in this country, it still has many bitter enemies here whose aim in life is the Church's subjection and destruction. They are doing all in their power to disfranchise Catholics by depriving them practically of the rights and privileges of American citizens. They even want to despoil Catholic parents of their natural right to educate their children according to the dictates of their conscience. These wicked men can succeed in their iniquitous and un-American endeavor only in one way, and that is, if Catholics neglect to use the weapon of defense given them by the constitution of our country. This weapon is the ballot. If Catholics use the ballot prudently, consistently, and universally, no one will ever reduce them to slavery; but once they grow careless in the employment

---

6 Note: Catholics cannot support any politician, Catholic or not, who supports intrinsically evil acts, such as abortion, euthanasia, homicide, and slavery as spelled out by *Gaudium et Spes*.

of this powerful weapon, it will be their own fault if they are subjected to an ignoble and tyrannical dominion. It devolves, therefore, upon our Catholic parents not only to vote themselves in the interest of our rights as American citizens—and to vote regularly at every election in order not to get out of the habit and be caught napping—but also to arrange that their children who are of age vote with them. In unity there is strength, especially with reference to the almighty ballot box of a nation like ours.

David and Goliath

The blatant bigotry rampant in various parts of our country may be likened to Goliath, the swaggering giant of the Philistines, flouting the chosen people of God and their religion. The pebble from the sling of David, that felled the mighty Goliath, is a symbol of the ballot. If all Catholics cast their vote with a true and sure aim at each election, the giant of intolerance, stalking abroad, will be reduced to impotence and disgrace.

But this treatise is mainly to deal with your vocation as married men and women; hence I shall now discourse on the subject of holy matrimony.

Chapter II

The Nature of Marriage

"And taking the right hand of his daughter, he gave it into the right hand of Tobias, saying: God . . . be with you, and may He join you together, and fulfill His blessing in you" (Tob. 7:15).

Instructing the first Christian married men and women regarding marriage, St. Paul said: "This is a great, sacrament: but I speak in Christ, and in the Church" (Eph. 5:32). Outside of the Church, notably in our country, matrimony is not only not treated as a sacrament, but it has really been degraded to a sort of a joke or a farce. Yet the Church upholds its sacredness as much as ever in the face of the neglect and ridicule of the world.

The God-Given Helpmate

God Himself instituted matrimony as the first and most binding human contract at the very beginning of the race.

After He created Adam and placed him in paradise, He said: "It is not good for man to be alone: let us make him a help like unto himself" (Gen. 2:18); and He created Eve to be Adam's helpmate. She was to help him attain his highest natural happiness and perfection, mentally, bodily, spiritually, emotionally, religiously, socially and in every other way; and he on his part was to render the same service to her. God intended this service to be bilateral, correlative, and reactive: each one was to achieve happiness and perfection by assisting the other party towards them. God made man and woman different from each other in body and mind, but not antagonistic; they were not to be mutually hostile and combative, but helpful and supplementary to one another: the one was to supply what the other lacked, not only as regards the body but also the soul. Where husband and wife have this correct conception of their relations and closely live up to them, they reach the greatest height of natural goodness, contentment, peace, and happiness. This is what God meant when He said: "It is not good for man to be alone: let us make him a help like unto himself." How utterly sad, that in so many instances the persons, who have been destined to be the grandest help and sweetest solace to one another, are mutually the heaviest handicap and the greatest kill-joy to each other!

Nature's Greatest Love

When God presented Eve to Adam as his wife, the latter grew inspired and exclaimed: "This now is bone of my bones, and flesh of my flesh. . . . Wherefore a man shall leave father and mother, and shall cleave to his wife: and they shall be two in one flesh" (Gen. 2:23–24). In these words Adam, speaking as the spokesman of God, evidently declares that the love between husband and wife is to be the strongest, the deepest, the most sacred, tender, and lasting love of nature. It was even to surpass the love of children for their parents. It was to be the God-given cement of the most holy and binding natural contract, which would give it the perpetuity and tenacity God intended it should have, namely, until death. How puny and insignificant are not all the other contracts of men aside of this sacred pact! In other contracts there is question of money, lands or other exchanged goods; in this contract there is a deal covering immortal beings in the most intimate and personal elements of life; and not only are the contracting parties concerned in the deal, but other immortal beings that are likely to spring directly or indirectly from this momentous union.

The Root of the Tree

For this reason, the Church insists so much on serious deliberation and the observance of all prudent cautions before this contract is ratified by the respective parties, since marriage not only affects them most closely and sensitively but is also the root of society at large. And as the nature of a tree depends largely upon the condition of its root, the Church postulates that the root of human society be kept clean, sound, and sacred. What a terrible contrast we find with this divine attitude of the Church in the nauseating antics of so many people today in our country, who pay more attention and are more careful when they make a bargain for a new automobile, or suit of clothes, or a pet dog, than when they choose their mate for life! They usually have to pay dearly for their frivolity and folly. God will not be mocked, and nature will not be trifled with.

Two in One

"They shall be two in one flesh." In these words the unity and indissolubility of marriage are proclaimed. This unity postulates that a man may simultaneously have but one wife, and a woman but one husband. Moreover this unity calls for unreserved harmony and unrestrained union of hearts and minds. Even as the physical union of husband

and wife are the closest possible, so, too, should their union of thought and sentiment be most intimate and complete. When a husband neglects his wife's physical or emotional needs or vice versa, there is a great temptation for the spouse to seek love outside of their marriage, which will never make the wayward spouse fulfilled. Since this is God's and nature's arrangement, it is easily understood why disloyalty in marriage, which prompts a man, for instance, to seek access to other women besides his wife, instead of procuring him more happiness, only mars the happiness he has; and why even pagan nations, led by the light of reason and common sense alone, are getting away from polygamy and are espousing monogamy as the only sound and solid marital condition of true happiness.

This unity and indissolubility of marriage, when duly reflected on, will make every candidate of marriage ponder and deliberate well and maturely before deciding on the choice of a mate; and after marriage they will make the partners of it very careful not to lose the love of the mate they have chosen. Before marriage they might have afforded to forfeit the love of this or that particular man or woman, since they could possibly have found a substitute. After marriage there can be no question of a substitute during the lifetime of the mate; if his or her love is lost, it cannot be replaced: hence the need of unity: "they shall be two in one flesh."

A Great Sacrament

In paradise God instituted marriage merely as a contract, but when our Lord came down upon this earth, He elevated it to the dignity of a sacrament. He made it one of the seven sacred channels through which His saving Blood was to flow upon the souls of men to sanctify them. As a sacrament, then, matrimony is holy as is baptism, Holy Eucharist, and Holy Orders. Our holy mother, the Church, evinces her high appreciation of matrimony by endowing its reception with a certain special solemnity. Baptism is usually administered outside the communion rail; so is penance; and when you receive Holy Communion or confirmation you kneel outside the sanctuary. But at marriage, provided it is celebrated in conjunction with Holy Mass, as I am supposing, the Church throws open the gates of the sanctuary, and introduces the candidates into the Holy of Holies, to the very spot where are offered the Body and Blood of Jesus Christ.

Love's Tragedy and Triumph

And why is holy marriage celebrated in connection with the Holy Sacrifice which, as we know, is the re-presentation of our Lord's death on the Cross? For this significant reason, that our Lord's death on Calvary was at the same time the greatest tragedy and the highest triumph of love. From it the candidates are to learn, at the very moment of their marriage, that their life, too, will be one of great and at times tremendous sacrifices, which for their virtuous endurance will draw on all the resources of their love, and that by this very endurance their mutual love will best show its genuineness and celebrate its finest triumphs. For true love reaches its zenith not in the sweet exchange of vows and professions of love, nor of mutual caresses and endearments: but in the cheerful embrace of labors and hardships, and in the glad submission to sacrifices and self-denials for the sake of the beloved one. The sooner the candidates of matrimony know this, the more they realize and the deeper they are imbued with this, the correct view of true love, the less disappointed and disillusioned they will likely be later on, and the happier and blessed will be their married life.

Holy matrimony is singular also for the fact that the parties to it are at the same time the ministers of it. The officiating priest is not the minister of the sacrament, but only the official witness of the Church to its administration. The groom and bride administer it mutually to one another and to themselves at the same time by the marriage consent. This reflection is also apt to give them a very high conception of the sacred contract they are entering.

Jesus at a Wedding

Our Lord worked His first public miracle at a wedding. He did this not by mere chance but designedly. To save a young married couple from worry and embarrassment, He changed water into wine; and the wine He provided was by far sweeter than the first wine they had had. Thereby our Savior indicated that He desired to be invited to every wedding of His followers; in other words, He wanted them to be married according to the laws of His Church, and in the state of sanctifying grace; and that upon their invitation He would be present not as an idle or uninterested spectator, but as the sponsor and guarantor of their marital happiness; so that in case the wine of their conjugal love would ever threaten to give out, or was actually exhausted, He could be counted on, provided they called on Him, to supply them with new love, which would often prove to be sweeter, stronger and more lasting than the first. Many couples, whose union suffered reverses in the first years of their married life, have experienced this to their consolation and happiness. And if there are among my readers men or women, whose married life is devoid of love and everything that approaches love, let them call with confidence upon the Lord for redress, and arrange with their mates to let go of the past, to begin their married life anew in God, and with His help to render it a perpetual and blissful honeymoon. The second wine at Cana was sweeter than the first, and it did not give out, but lasted to the very end of the feast. The Lord is good to those who love Him. And a trustful prayer to Mary will induce her to repeat her wondrous intercessory feat of Cana in your and your spouse's favor.

Are You Really Married?

You are married. Have you been married according to the laws of the Church? If not, yours is not a lawful marriage, but merely a sinful relation with a person who is not your mate. By elevating marriage to the dignity of a sacrament, Christ gave the Church exclusive charge over the marriage of His followers. As little power as the state or other external agents have over the administration of Holy Communion, for instance, or Holy Orders, so little right have they over the sacrament of matrimony. The Catholic who attempts marriage before a non-Catholic minister is by that very deed excommunicated or expelled from the Church.[7] From this excommunication the penitent can be absolved only by the bishop or by a priest delegated by the bishop.

---

7 To get married at a non-Catholic Church or have a non-Catholic minister preside, the Catholic spouse must seek permission from his bishop. This is called a "dispensation from canonical form." See Can. 1124 and Can. 1125 for more details.

In case you have not been legitimately married, and your union is capable of adjustment, have it righted, the sooner the better. Why unnecessarily prolong your estrangement from God, your remorse of conscience, and your great risk of losing eternal salvation? The process will not be so hard and disagreeable as you imagine. You will find your pastor and the bishop considerate, sympathetic, and kind. Do not hesitate or delay, therefore, to consult the peace of your mind and the welfare of your immortal soul. "Behold, now is the acceptable time, behold, now is the day of salvation" (2 Cor. 6:2). Whatever humiliation or mortification may be demanded of you in the procedure, you ought to endure cheerfully in atonement of the sin you committed by your sinful attempt of marriage, and as the price of a good conscience.

A Sacrament of the Living

You say, however, that you have been married in keeping with the requirements of the Church; you were married, perhaps, with considerable ceremony. Were you in the state of grace when you married? Matrimony is a sacrament of the living, and the recipient must not be conscious of an unforgiven mortal sin.[8] There are those who before mar-

8 Three conditions must be met for a sin to be considered mortal: grave matter, full knowledge and complete consent.

riage, in the period of courtship, sin flagrantly with each other by indulging in, or allowing improprieties, indecent liberties and shocking intimacies. When they go to confession before marriage, they are ashamed or too proud to confess these mortal sins. They willfully make an invalid confession, receive Holy Communion unworthily, and are married validly, indeed, yet sacrilegiously. No wonder that they do not receive the grace of the sacrament, and that their married life is unhappy in consequence. They started it altogether wrong, even with the curse of God. What are they to do to set matters right?

Where There's a Will, There's a Way

All they need to do is to make a good general confession covering the entire period from their last worthy confession to the present time. This confession is not at all hard for those who have the will to get back to God. The priest will give you what help you need, supposing you are in this plight. And do not believe you are the first one to tell this story to the priest. It is by no means new to him. He has heard it often before, and he will hear it again in the future. Human nature is always the same everywhere. So take heart and speak honestly in the spirit of true and humble contrition. Then, when you receive absolution, you will get not only the graces of holy penance, but also those of matrimony. They have been and are only suspended, waiting for the hindrance of mortal sin to be removed from your soul. No sooner the hindrance is gone, the suspension will cease, and the graces of marriage will flood, strengthen and rejoice your soul.

Chapter III
The Purposes and Privileges of Marriage

"O Lord, give me understanding, and I will search Thy law; and I will keep it with my whole heart" (Ps. 118:33, 34).

Marriage has been instituted by God for three purposes. It is mandatory to attend to these purposes to have the right view of matrimony, and to know what it allows and disallows to husband and wife. Before I go any further I want to caution my readers that my subject will now grow very delicate. I shall have to deal with very personal and intimate sexual matters that are not discussed or even mentioned in public, except in the time of a mission before audiences made up of married people exclusively.

Many Catholics dislike to hear the priest speak on these topics at all. They pretend to be much shocked at it, and say it ill becomes him and his sacred dignity, and that in a holy place, to make mention of such things. They ask, moreover: "What does he, an unmarried man, know of the intimacies of marriage? where does he get his knowledge? and what business has he, anyway, to meddle with people's most private affairs? It is an affront and imposition, that's all." When Catholics speak thus, it is usually due to only one reason: an uneasy conscience. They feel guilty, and they do not want their remorses and self-reproaches to be increased in number and kind and force. Hence their bitter and virulent criticism of the unwelcome and candid monitor.

The Stupid Ostrich

Frequently, Catholic married couples purposely stay away from the special instruction for the married during a mission in order not to have their false and treacherous calm of conscience, regarding their heinous sins against matrimony, disturbed. Even as the ostrich is said to hide his head in the sand when the hunters are hot on his trail, so these deluded sinners try to blind themselves to the wrath of God that will be sure to overtake them if they do not repent.

The Physician of the Soul

Conscientious Catholic married men and women are grateful for whatever instruction and information is given them regarding the sacred relations of married life. They want to do only what is right. In order to do it, they have to know it. Who is to tell them what is right or wrong in the conduct of marriage if not the priest, their God-given guide and teacher? In whom else could they have confidence in matters of conscience? Where does the priest get this knowledge? It is imparted to him in his long years of study preparatory to his elevation to the priesthood, and it is increased and clarified by his observations and his multiple and varied experiences in the holy ministry. The knowledge which the physician requires to attend to the health of the body, the priest respectively needs to look after the welfare of the soul. Before marriage, it is difficult, if not practically impossible, to give the young candidates all the knowledge they ought to have with reference to the ethics of married life; hence young married couples are particularly appreciative of solid information in this regard.

"All Things Are Clean to the Clean"

It is furthermore to be observed, that there is nothing intrinsically bad in nature, notably in the human body, and in the marriage relations of husband and wife. The human body is created by God just as it is with all its parts and organs: consequently it is good altogether, for God cannot create anything bad. And every part of the body is consecrated to God as His temple, and as the dwelling-place of the Holy Ghost, through holy baptism. In its completeness it is blessed again and again by the Church, and after the Consecration in the nuptial Mass the bride's body receives a particular blessing with regard to the sexual life. Our Lord, becoming man, assumed the human body just as it is in its entirety, and He gave it, too, to His ever-Blessed Mother. Of itself, then, neither the human body nor any of its parts is bad. It only becomes bad when it is used or abused and misused for purposes not sanctioned by God. Here apply the words of St. Paul: "All things are clean to the clean: but to them that are defiled . . . nothing is clean: but both their mind and their conscience are defiled" (Titus 1:15).

For the Glory of God

The marital relations have been expressly instituted and ordained by God: hence they, too, are not bad but, if they are performed in keeping with God's ordinance, they are good and holy. St. Paul exhorts the first Christians to keep their "marriage honorable in all, and the bed undefiled" (Hebr. 13:4), meaning that the lawful use of marriage leaves no moral stain whatever in its wake. And of the married woman the same Apostle says: "She shall be saved by bearing children, if she continue in faith, and love, and sanctification with sobriety" (1 Tim. 2:15). Since a woman cannot bear children without submitting to the marriage duty, St. Paul indirectly assures her that she can even use it, provided she yields to it in keeping with God's law, as a means of her salvation and sanctification. Far from being something vile, filthy, and vulgar, the marriage act, properly performed, is holy and pleasing in the eyes of God, and merits an increase of glory in heaven. It falls fully and without any reservation under the classification given by St. Paul in these words: "Therefore, whether you eat or drink, or whatsoever else you do; do all things for the glory of God" (1 Cor. 10:31). This, then, is the genuine Catholic conception of the marriage act. All Catholic married couples ought to view it in this light always; for nothing will contribute more to keep them "in faith, and love, and sanctification with sobriety." Such being the case, it is evident that we can discuss the intimacies of marriage with all due delicacy and reverence for its high and sacred character.

Three Purposes of Marriage

The three purposes for which God instituted holy marriage are, first, the reproduction or multiplication of the human race. He no sooner joined the first couple in matrimony when He "blessed them, saying: Increase and multiply, and fill the earth" (Gen. 1:28). St. Francis de Sales says that marriage is to fill the earth with good citizens, and people heaven with saints: a most worthy purpose, to be sure. In the second place matrimony is to foster mutual love and attachment between husband and wife. Finally, it is destined to serve as a sedative to concupiscence, or the sexual passion. In themselves passions are not bad, but good. There would be no motive power in human nature and in human society without them, and nothing good would be achieved. They are bad only when they are perverted to ends prohibited by God. The strongest passion in man is the desire for food and drink. The next strongest is the sexual passion. The one aims at the preservation of the individual, the other at that of the race. Both are very necessary, as is evident; and as good as they are necessary. To give the sexual passion virtuous and honorable satisfaction God instituted holy marriage.

Practical Corollaries

From all that has been said we can deduce certain practical corollaries regarding the intimate life of husband and wife. Above all the marriage act so-called, or the sexual intercourse of husband and wife, is not only tolerated but is directly ordained by God; hence lawful, respectable, and sacred; for without it the human family cannot increase as declared by God. The marital act is justified by any of the three purposes mentioned above. It frequently happens that the first purpose, the procreation of children, is out of question, either because the woman is already pregnant, or because she is beyond the child-bearing age, or for some other reason; yet one or the other, or both of the two remaining purposes of marriage warrant the act. Nor is it necessary that married couples be conscious of, or directly intend the purposes of matrimony when they have knowledge of one another; it is sufficient if they have a mind to perform conscientiously the duties of their state life.

Enough Is Too Much

How often is the marriage act allowed? This depends upon the will and choice of the parties concerned. The only restriction is that of moderation, which must be observed in all things. Common sense and a healthy self-love together with the law of God counsel moderation. Eating and drinking furnish an illustration here. We are not told how many meals we may eat a day. This is left to our judgment. But if one is intemperate in the consumption of food, and attempts, let us say, to eat six full meals a day, he will soon destroy his very capacity to take food at all, and with it every appetite for food and all enjoyment in its partaking. What was designed to give him pleasure only produces nausea and disgust in him. This is nature's punishment for intemperance. It is relatively the same with regard to immoderation in connubial indulgence. It soon brings its own penalty, not only in the way of corporal weakness and disease, but it also produces a certain estrangement, coldness and disgust between the parties who are guilty of it. In carnal gratifications particularly is verified the saying: Enough is too much. Beware of surfeiting yourself if you want the capacity for reasonable enjoyment to continue. Greater happiness is achieved, and sweeter thrills are enjoyed by virtuously restraining, than by wildly indulging, the desires of the flesh.

In Moderation Is Happiness

Perhaps this marital intemperance accounts more than anything else for the sad but frequent observation that husband and wife easily tire of and grow apart from each other when they should still be in the very height of their honeymoon. The reason why they are mutually wearied and bored by one another is often because in their newly married life they have over-emphasized the lure of the flesh, and yielded to it without the wholesome restraint of virtue and good sense. While man is perhaps the guiltier party in this excess as a rule, the woman is frequently as guilty or even more guilty than he by her immoderate craving for sensible caresses and emotional endearments. If, through motives of virtue and discretion, both man and wife moderate their penchant for carnal delights and passionate thrills, they will be richly compensated for this renouncement by a greater tenderness, a sweeter devotion, and a deeper, a more even, and a more lasting attachment to one another. There is not only virtue but also good common sense in following the advice of the Apostle who says: "Everyone of you should know how to possess his vessel in sanctification and honor: not in the passion of lust like the Gentiles that know not God" (1 Thess. 4:4, 5).

The Spirit Is Above the Flesh

It is a low level of marital happiness, indeed, which finds its greatest expression in the relations of the flesh; and it is doomed to be as short-lived as it is shallow. Wise and virtuous Christian couples derive their highest joys from the sources of their mutual friendship, esteem, and homage, and from the exchange of sentiments of, and stimulations to, virtue, honor, and goodness. The woman, particularly, will remember to her profit that if she is going to hold the sincere respect, the high regard, and the tender reverence of her husband, which to every honorable married woman means so much for her ease and well-being, she must always observe a certain feminine delicacy and modest reserve even in the most intimate familiarities of marriage; for man is by nature so constituted that even when he permits himself every sexual excess, he still cannot respect a woman who shamelessly throws off every restraint and forfeits all the charming elusiveness and fascinating mystery with which nature has endowed her for her protection from, as well as for her power over man. And every honorable, chivalrous, and truly gallant husband tenderly respects and carefully guards his wife's innate love of purity and instinct of modesty. He avoids everything in his own conduct that might shock or revolt her intimate sensibilities.

The Children of Saints

Both husband and wife, from the very beginning of their married life, will bear in mind that sooner or later the time will come when for certain reasons marital abstinence will be imposed upon them as a duty, say in the period of sickness or the absence of one of the parties, or because an increase in the family is at the time undesirable.[9] They will

9 The Church allows married couples to use Natural Family Planning (NFP) for "serious" or "just reasons," which include physical, economic, and social conditions. NFP involves periodic continence.

be more capable of rendering this duty then, the more they practiced themselves in moderation from the start of their nuptial life. They ought to take heart in the words of the angel Raphael to Tobias: "Hear me, and I will show thee who they are, over whom the devil can prevail. For they who in such manner receive matrimony, as to shut out God from themselves, and from their mind, and to give themselves to their lust, as the horse and mule, which have not understanding, over them the devil hath power" (Tob. 6:16–17). The night after their marriage, Tobias exhorted the virgin (his wife), and said to her: "Sara, arise, and let us pray to God today, and tomorrow and the next day: because for these three nights we are joined to God: and when the third night is over, we will be in our own wedlock. For we are the children of saints, and we must not be joined together like heathens that know not God. So they both arose, and prayed earnestly both together that health might be given them. . . . Sara also said: Have mercy on us, O Lord, have mercy on us, and let us grow old both together in health" (Tob. 8:4 sqq.).

Voluntary Abstinence

There are no days on which the marriage duty is prohibited. Pious couples at times by mutual consent abstain from nuptial converse in advent and lent, on Sundays, holydays, and Communion days; but this is optional on their part, not obligatory. The Church desires married people also to communicate daily as much as possible; yet the Church does not want Catholics to die out for lack of progeny: hence the marriage duty is evidently permitted on Communion days. This will not appear surprising at all if we remember that the act is good, virtuous, and sacred when performed in keeping with the ordinance of God. During the time of the woman's menstruation, the husband's instinct, in addition to his consideration for his wife's health, will counsel abstinence. In the Old Law this abstinence was enjoined on the husband.

Certain Inferences

The marriage act being good and sacred, whatever contributes to render it more pleasurable, and consequently more efficient, in a virtuous manner, by way of preparation and accompaniment, is also permitted; even as it can give savor and spice to food in order to make it more appetizing and, as a result, more nourishing. Married people are justly entitled to all the delight they can reasonably procure from the marital act, for they pay fully for this delight by the assumption of its consequences and the attendant responsibilities; hence they need not scruple on that score. Moreover, whatever one is justified in doing, he may also dwell on in thought and desire and discuss with the proper party; inferentially husband and wife may think of, and desire, and discuss with one another what they are at liberty to do with one another. Of course, if such thoughts, imaginations, desires, and discussions would aim at, or cause voluntary self-abuse, or expose their subject to a proximate danger of it, they would be sinful.

Further Corollaries

In addition to the marriage act there are other sexual privileges accorded married people. Certain marks of endearment and demonstrations of love, such as kisses, embraces, caresses, looks, touches and the like, which for single people might be grievously immodest and mortally sinful, are not only allowed between husband and wife, but, in view of the purposes of marriage, they are even virtuous and good. It is impossible to go into further details in this matter here, but a married person can safely follow this principle as to what is, or is not allowed in the marriage relations: as long as husband and wife in their mutual sexual behavior do not intentionally or consciously cause ejaculation in themselves or the other party before intercourse, or willfully expose themselves to the proximate danger of it: whatever they may do to foster or show mutual love, and however it is done, is not in itself sinful. There may be a degree of immoderation there and, therefore, a venial sin; but the acts of themselves are not sinful since, as we are supposing, they serve the purposes of holy matrimony either directly or indirectly. Immoderation, however, either as to the nature or manner of the sexual conduct between husband and wife, should be jealously avoided. It may start as a venial fault, and by and by grow to serious dimensions, and run into gross excesses and shameful immorality.

Ask the Priest

If there remains to you a doubt in this important matter of married life, ask the priest in the confessional for the information you require. As was said before, this subject can be treated and discussed modestly and reverently. The priest will be glad to enlighten you for the peace of your mind and the welfare of your soul. If you submit delicate matters concerning your bodily health to the physician of the body, why should you shrink from submitting delicate matters regarding your spiritual health to the physician of the soul? Is not the health of the soul more valuable than that of the body? Do not be afraid; you are not the first one to ask the priest the question you are troubled with.

No doubt you feel, and I fully agree, that it is quite unusual for a priest to discuss these intimate matters so frankly as I am doing: but the fact is that many Catholic married couples are in considerable ignorance as to their duties and privileges in this important element of married life; many consider to be sinful what is perfectly harmless; and others see no harm in things that are grossly sinful: hence the need of enlightenment, and the appreciation of it on the part of those who want to save their souls in holy matrimony.

The Final Caution

After having told what is lawful in marriage, I must once more add the caution that husband and wife will be wise in always behaving in such a manner towards each other that, while they tender one another the desirable expressions of genuine and ardent conjugal love, they never forfeit for one another the high respect and delicate regard which are so valuable an asset of the happiness of marriage. Even married people can get to know one another too well, and become too intimate for their own good.

In married life, too, undue familiarity breeds contempt. And this is true not only as to the sexual life, but also with reference to the other relations of husband and wife. In a certain way, as regards the sweet and delicate courtesies, amenities, and civilities of their daily converse, they ought to always behave as strangers to each other in the sense that they continue to try to make and maintain the best possible impression upon one another, the husband being the perfect gentleman, and the wife being the perfect lady, with all that these terms imply, mutually to one another in the seclusion and sanctuary of their little home. Then neither will take too much for granted, or hurt, let alone outrage, the finer sensibilities of the other through bad manners, untidiness, discourteousness, not to speak of coarseness or vulgarity. St. Francis de Sales says a gentleman or a lady are such even when alone; hence it is not expecting too much to ask them to be such when they are joined in the sweet and sacred relations of husband and wife. It may be hard to maintain the role throughout, but it pays wonderfully.

St. Gregory, too, gives valuable advice when he reminds us that the best way to keep oneself from doing what is unlawful is to abstain immediately from what is lawful. Married people will find this custom, if they apply it prudently in the use of marriage, to be a wonderful preservative of the sweet and substantial happiness of marriage. By here and there denying themselves what they may do, they forestall the risk of sometimes doing what they must not do.

Chapter IV

Sins Against Holy Marriage

Part One

"For how knowest thou, O wife, whether thou shalt save thy husband? Or how knowest thou, O man, whether thou shalt save thy wife? But as the Lord hath distributed to every one. . . . so let him walk" (Cor. 7:16).

I have been speaking of the rights and privileges of marriage. Now I must address the disagreeable duty of pointing out the offenses done against holy matrimony. I want to repeat what I emphasized at the beginning of this lecture that whatever I am going to say is not to make you feel miserable, depressed, discouraged, or cheap, as the common expression is: but it will aim only at your instruction, encouragement, betterment, and salvation. And right here I want to say that I shall be able to mention no sin, however and how often done, for which there is not an immediate and complete remedy at hand in the sacrament of holy penance, provided the perpetrator sincerely repents of the sin, and is minded never to repeat it again.

The Violation of Nature

There are married couples who commit the solitary sin, also called masturbation, pollution, or self-abuse. They contracted this sin possibly before marriage and continue the practice of it after marriage. This is a mortal sin, for married couples as well as for the unmarried; for marriage gives no right to abuse nature. In a way this sin is greater in married couples because the use of marriage serves them as a virtuous outlet for concupiscence, and thus renders the solitary sin in them more heinous.

"Defraud Not One Another"

Married people sin by refusing the other party the marriage right or duty when a *reasonable* request or demand is made for it. This refusal is a grievous sin, because a serious right of another is being denied, without sufficient cause, as we are supposing. If there is more of a mere suggestion or hint than a real demand in the request that is made for the marriage act, and the party has no mind to assert or urge his or her right to it, and is quite satisfied to take a negative answer, the declension of the request is not a sin. But if the party is in earnest in making the request or demand, and there is no solid reason for non-compliance, it is a grave sin to refuse.[10]

Perhaps women are more guilty of this sin than men, as a rule. Nature accounts for this. Men are by nature more passionate than women. Their sexual life is more eager for expression. Then, too, they no doubt ordinarily derive greater pleasure and more satisfaction from the marriage act than women. For some women, this act is not only not pleasurable but positively painful and decidedly repellent. This may not be normal, but it is a fact. When they arrive at the age of forty quite a number of married women, who derived considerable pleasure from the act in their younger years, seem naturally to be weaned from it to lose all interest in, and desire for it. They prefer to do without it and forget about it entirely for life; not that it causes them positive pain, but it simply lacks appeal or attraction for them. Their desire is to live with their husband as sister and brother, and to eschew all connubial relations for the rest of their life. The most common cause why women are more apt than men to shrink from the marriage act is, because the act is likely in the way of generation to have

10 Note: A spouse can refuse the marital act if the person asking for intercourse is intoxicated, one spouse is sick, or there is danger to the unborn child or other similar reasons. However, charity beckons the spouses to be reasonable in their request.

consequences that mean more to the woman, and tax her immensely more than man. These and other reasons of an emotional and temperamental nature account for the fact that women are more likely than men to be guilty of the sin of marital refusal.

For Better or for Worse

But a good woman always reflects that she took her husband not only for better, but also for worse; not only for pleasure, but also for pain. St. Paul told the first Christian couples: "Let the husband render the debt to his wife, and the wife also in like manner to the husband. The wife hath not power of her own body, but the husband. And in like manner the husband also hath not power of his own body, but the wife. Defraud not one another, except, perhaps, by consent, for a time, that you may give yourselves to prayer; and return together again, lest Satan tempt you for your incontinency. But I speak this by indulgence, not by commandment" (1 Cor. 7:3 sqq.).

In nothing are husband and wife mutually so dependent on one another as in procuring the legitimate satisfaction of their sexual needs. Wherever the reciprocal sexual enjoyment of one another is justly, lovingly, and virtuously arranged, by mutual understanding, sympathetic considerateness, and sensible moderation, the first love of married life is not only maintained, but continually fostered and increased. And this love, nursed in this manner, renders the endurance of the greatest ordeals and the severest trials of marriage easy and sweet. By periodically reawakening the sexual appetite and the mutual desire for each other in married couples nature provides them with an unfailing source of reciprocal dependence on, attachment to, and a virtuous relish of one another. This is nature's own plan. To disturb or interfere with it through selfishness or other mean motives is pure folly, and is sure to invite conjugal displeasure, coldness, estrangement, and bitterness.

"Debt" and "Tribulations"

The Apostle calls the marriage act a "debt," implying that it would at times be a real and painful burden, as the payment of a debt frequently is; and yet it must be paid, if possible; similarly the marriage duty must be rendered at the desire of the other party, even at a sacrifice. Many a married woman on Judgment Day will be assigned her place among the adulteresses to her everlasting confusion and chagrin, not because she committed adultery herself, but because by refusing him his marriage rights she indirectly caused her husband to look elsewhere for his sexual gratification, and she thus became an accomplice of his sin. The husband, of course, is never justified in having recourse to an adulterous connection, even when he is refused his sacred rights at home; but the refusing wife will be about as guilty as he is himself, for having practically driven him to sin. The same is true regarding her guilt in the sin of self-abuse, to which the husband may resort in the case under consideration. Before she marries, a woman should well ponder on the words of St. Paul: "If a virgin marry, she . . . shall have tribulation of the flesh" (1 Cor. 7:28). After marriage her obligation is, in spite of these tribulations, which are often severe, to pay her debt to her husband.

The Golden Rule

In every phase of married life, but particularly in this feature of it, both parties should always bear in mind the words of the Apostle: "Bear ye one another's burdens: and so you shall fulfill the law of Christ" (Gal. 6:2). In other words, true sympathy, by which one can make every allowance for the other's feelings, penchants, weaknesses and needs, and imagine himself or herself in the condition of the other, and is inclined to treat the other as he or she would like to be treated in the same condition, will inspire the proper conduct on all occasions. The woman on her part will remember that man is by nature more passionate than she is, and she will be glad to yield to him for his pleasure, even though she suffers but pain. And the man on his part will bear in mind that woman is sexually different from man, and often feels revulsion where he experiences desire, and he will generously, magnanimously, and unselfishly restrain his own appetite as much as possible in favor of his wife's comfort and well-being. Here especially he often has a chance to display true love in its highest form: he will deny himself what he craves most to please the one he loves most on earth.[11]

Selfishness Does Not Invite Sacrifice

In many instances the husband is the cause of his wife's reluctance to perform the marriage duty because of his selfish or even brutal manner. He evinces no tenderness, affection, devotion or love for his wife, but only looks for the gratification of his sensuous passion. This attitude revolts a woman of a delicate temperament and fine sensibilities. She feels that she is entitled to more consideration than merely to serve as an object of animal passion. She wants to be on a higher plane in the esteem of her husband, and inspire in him nobler sentiments than merely those of the horse and the mule, as the Bible puts it. Where the better and finer

---

11 Pope St. John Paul II said a husband can commit the sin of lust against his own wife (Matt. 5:27–28). A virtuous husband must never use his wife as an object, but as "my sister, my spouse," (Sg. 4:9)—his helpmate to heaven.

feelings, and their prudent and tactful demonstration are not lacking in a man for his wife, the woman will seldom be unwilling to yield to him in marriage.

Of course it happens, too, at times, that a man is guilty of the refusal of the marriage duty towards his wife; if not directly—for from delicacy the woman may shrink from making a formal request—yet indirectly; for although he knows that his wife is desirous of enjoying her marriage rights, he treats her coldly and ignores her and her desires, from a feeling of spite or revenge, or from a certain coldness, moodiness or what not. At any rate he falls seriously short of his wedding contract with her, since he does not place his body at her disposal as he ought, and he commits a grave sin, and is inferentially a partner to whatever sins of adultery or self-abuse she may resort to in consequence.

Here it may be observed that a long, willful and unjustifiable absence from one another may involve the same grievous sins for the guilty party as a positive refusal of the marriage debt.

Exemptions and Excuses

The reasons which excuse from the obligation of rendering the marriage duty are various. Above all, if one party commits adultery, and this is established beyond question, it thereby permanently forfeits all its right to the marital act, and the innocent party need never render it again. This is the theory, and strict justice.[12] Yet the innocent party will usually consider whether forgiveness will not be more called for than insistence on absolute justice; especially when it reflects on the words of Jesus: "Forgive, and you shall be forgiven. For with the same measure that you shall mete withal, it shall be measured to you again" (Luke 6:37–38). By one carnal intercourse after it obtained knowledge of the crime committed by the partner, the innocent party condones it forever, and may never again allege it as a cause for the refusal of the marriage duty; unless, of course, the other would repeat the sin of adultery after the condonation of it.

Actual serious illness, or a well-grounded fear of contracting a serious disease, are sufficient reasons to decline the nuptial request, for in this supposition it would not be reasonable, as it always must be to deserve recognition. The same holds good if, because of the time or place, there is danger of scandal; or if the request is altogether immoderate in its frequency, and is consequently unreasonable of itself, and is likely to prove injurious to the body and mind of one or both parties. In all things nature has certain limits which are never transgressed with impunity. The request of

12 Some saints like St. Monica and Bl. Elizabeth Mora helped bring about their husband's conversion after their infidelity, making it part of their life's mission to pray for their salvation.

a drunken mate need not be honored, for it is unreasonable, and a child conceived in the period of intoxication of one of the parents starts its existence on this earth with a handicap. If a man grossly neglects to support his family properly, his wife is justified in refusing the marriage duty until he changes his conduct; for it is unreasonable to ask her to bring children into the world while he evidently has no mind to provide for them. In cases of doubt in this very serious and delicate matter, it is wise to submit the case candidly to one's confessor; in the meanwhile it is usually better and wiser to yield at a sacrifice rather than to risk withholding a right belonging to another.

Chapter V

Sins Against Holy Marriage

Part Two

"Lord, Thou knowest, that not for fleshly lust do I take . . . a wife, but only for the sake of posterity, in which Thy Name may be blessed for ever and ever" (Tob. 8:9).

The sin I am now going to mention is among married people perhaps the most common on the one hand, and the most insidious on the other; it is insidious because it is common, and it is common because it is insidious.[13] It is unfortunately making greater inroads into the Catholic population of our country from day to day, and its fatal virus seems preferably to inoculate the Catholics who in a worldly sense are having success and prosperity, who get up in the world and shine in society. In other words, when

13 The sin of pornography was not addressed in this section but in the publisher's note. In our digital age, the scourge of pornography is wreaking havoc on marriages.

Catholics have more reason to thank God for His goodness towards them, they appear inclined to serve Him less. His great goodness often makes them meanly selfish.

The Sin of Many Names

The sin I have reference to goes by countless names. It is called birth control, race suicide, contraception, the sin of prevention, of being careful, of improper marital relations, of withdrawal, of mutual self-abuse, of wasting nature, of spilling the seed, and the like. In theological parlance it is spoken of as onanism, so called after Onan, who is mentioned in the first book of the Bible as having committed this terrible sin. It is perpetrated variously; yet the purpose is always the same, namely to prevent conception whilst performing the rites of marriage. Sometimes the man, then again the woman uses an instrument that renders conception impossible during the marriage relations; at times, too, the woman, immediately after the intercourse employs the syringe or interior douche to achieve the same object. Whatever is done, and however it is done: when nature is purposely defeated of its design in marriage, whilst the privileges of matrimony are being enjoyed, the parties concerned are guilty of mortal sin every time they thus wantonly waste the God-given powers of nature.

Nature Is Outraged

I say "every time"; for there never can be any justification for this act under any circumstances imaginable. It is an unnatural act, or a sin against nature: hence of itself, and in its very essence detestable and wicked. No priest, no bishop, no pope can declare it lawful or excusable in any condition or conjuncture of life. God Himself cannot give anyone the faculty to commit such an act, since it is contrary to nature; and God, the author of nature, cannot militate against Himself. No stress of poverty, therefore, no delicacy of constitution on the part of the woman, no prediction of the doctor as to her sure death if she should attempt to bring another child into the world, no siege of disease on the part of the breadwinner of the family and consequent economical struggle: in a word, no reason whatsoever is or can be a just cause for the conduct referred to: for what is intrinsically unnatural can never be rendered allowed or tolerable.

The Vomitorium of the Romans

The primary natural purpose of the marriage act is the procreation of offspring. It is therefore obviously unnatural to perform the act in such a way as to frustrate this purpose. An illustration may again be taken from the satisfaction of the first and strongest human passion, the appetite for food. The first purpose of the consumption of food is nourishment of the body. To obstruct this purpose willfully while eating or drinking is an unnatural misdemeanor. The old Romans, in the height of their luxury, are recorded to have been guilty of this sin. At their sumptuous banquets they would eat unto satiety, and forthwith they would use a feather or some other means to disgorge at once everything they had eaten, so they could begin to eat soon again. Everybody instinctively feels that this was an outrage of nature, which intends, not that the pleasure of eating be an end in itself, but that it contributes to the health and maintenance of the body; hence such a brutish behavior is extremely nauseating. Yet it is no different from the abuse of nature that is perpetrated by sinful birth control, in which the mere pleasure of the marriage act is sought to the willful exclusion of the very purpose of the pleasure. Nature has a very distinct end in view in attaching so vehement a pleasure to the marriage act; and whoever frustrates this end while reaping the pleasure contravenes nature, and will sooner or later suffer its revenge. Nature is a hard creditor, and is inexorable in its demand of full payment for every outrage committed against it. The very fact that animals, which are guided by the instinct of nature throughout, never resort to this abominable practice is additional evidence that it is against nature, and consequently worse than brutish.

"A Detestable Thing"

God's invariable attitude towards the sin of contraception is clearly delineated in the book of Genesis (38:8 sqq.). You will not take it amiss if I describe it to you in the very words of the Bible. The brother of Onan had died without leaving issue. "Juda therefore said to Onan his son: Go into thy brother's wife and marry her, that thou mayest raise seed to thy brother. He knowing that the children should not be his, when he went into his brother's wife, spilled his seed upon the ground, lest children should be born in his brother's name. And therefore the Lord slew him because he did a detestable thing." That happened about four thousand years ago. Since then, however, the nature of the sin has not changed, and God is still the same. Nor does it make a bit of difference that this sin is widespread and quite universally practiced. It remains the same detestable thing, and provokes the same anger of God. At the time of Sodom and Gomorrah and, anteriorly, of the deluge, practically everybody indulged in the excesses of the flesh: yet the universality did not diminish, let alone disarm, the wrath of God.

"A Blessing and a Curse"

As He said to the Jews of old, God says as it were to the married couple at the very beginning of their nuptial life: "Behold I set forth in your sight this day a blessing and a curse: a blessing, if you obey the commandments of the Lord your God, which I command you this day: a curse, if you obey not the commandments of the Lord your God, but revolt from the way which now I show you" (Deut. 11:26–28). If they intend to use their marriage rights He offers them the invaluable blessing of good and healthy children, who will be their joy, consolation, and pride, who will cement more and more their conjugal love, and represent its best and most precious fruit.[14] But in case they refuse this blessing, God threatens them with His curse: the curse of misfortune and disease, the curse of ill-luck and poverty, the curse of mutual estrangement and domestic infelicity, the curse of lukewarmness in the faith and of a sacrilegious reception of the sacraments, the curse, often, of complete and final apostasy from the Church, and absolute defection from God.

---

[14] Note: children are a gift and not a right. God does not owe any couple good and healthy children. Sometimes, a couple might be blessed with a child with special needs, who will help them get to heaven.

Renegades and Hypocrites

Everywhere there are renegade Catholics. In consideration of the excellent Catholic parents and education they have had, one wonders what ever could have alienated them to such a degree from the Church of their fathers as to fill them with a veritable hatred for it, so much so that they purposely avoid passing a church or meeting a priest or a nun on the street in order not to be reminded of it. When they were young men or young women, they were good and pious. For the life of them they would never have willfully received a sacrament unworthily. But alas, when they married, they were soon engulfed by the current of sensuality and the relinquishment of marital duty prevalent on all sides. They yielded to their selfish craving for nuptial indulgence dissociated from the sacred responsibilities of it. They knew they were doing wrong as they began to violate nature, but they used all kinds of fleshly remedies to dull their conscience and lull it to sleep. They either made no mention at all these mortal sins in the confessional, and lied to the Holy Ghost; or, if they mentioned them, it was without genuine sorrow and a firm purpose of amendment. Their confession was invalid and a sacrilege; and the consequent Holy Communion was another sacrilege. Heaping sin upon sin, and sacrilege upon sacrilege, their conscience soon became so hopelessly involved and restless that they could no longer endure the disharmony between the voice of God in them and their life, between their religious profession and their conduct: until they gradually decided to put an end to their mental and spiritual torture by giving up the practice of their faith entirely and forever. And after this step it was not long before they got so far away from God as though they had never known Him or heard of Him. When they give the reasons for their apostasy, asked or unasked, they like to throw the blame upon this or that priest, in or out of the confessional: whereas the real cause of it was their detestable conduct in marriage, and the fulfilment of the tremendous threat of God that, if they refused His blessing, He would inflict upon them His curse. God will not be mocked.

Foolish Subterfuges

In the light of this we know how to appraise the conduct of those who say, for instance, that they are desiring to have a child or two someday, but not right away after their marriage; for they want to go out a lot at first and have a good time; when they have enough of that they will be willing to settle down and have a little family. God deals with such young couples in His own way. If they use the rights of marriage but are unwilling to accept the children He offers them, He may not repeat the offer later when they are not only willing but most eager to have children. He will say, so to speak: "When I was willing to give you children, you iniquitously refused them; now that you want them, you shall not have them." No one can fool God. There are others who do not want the children close together; others again who know exactly just how many children they can take care of and educate properly according to their circumstances, and they will accept no more; usually the number is very small, consisting of one or two; there are those, too, who say they are too old to think of having additions to the family, and they would be rather embarrassed by the experience; quite many have been told by some doctor or other that another child will spell death to the mother. In the meantime, however, they continue sinfully to exploit the nuptial relations to their sensuous delight. They give to the flesh what belongs to the flesh, but not to God what belongs to God.

"Judge Not!"

Here the caution is in season, that we must not judge others by mere appearances. We can be very uncharitable and unfair in blaming or even only suspecting them of sinful practices, just because they have no children, or but one or two after many years of married life, or because the children are far apart in years. "They must be taking precaution," meddlesome and gossipy people are inclined to say. Indeed, they are taking precaution, but often this is virtuous rather than sinful. There are many childless couples whose main earthly desire is to be blessed with children. They pray fervently for this boon daily. For reasons of His own God withholds or delays the granting of their request. Meanwhile with the affliction of childlessness they have to bear the injury of being misunderstood and unjustly blamed.

Other couples, who have but one or two children, or have more children with considerable intervals of time between them, are using precaution, too. They live together in virtuous continency and conjugal abstinence when they feel they dislike another increase in the family for the time being.[15] There are more married people practicing this at times heroic self-discipline than the world knows of, or would be ready to believe, were it told of it. At first they find it hard, of course; but with the help of prayer and the regular, at least monthly, worthy reception of the sacraments, and through mutual encouragement in self-restraint, they soon find the virtuous practice easy and sweet, increasing in them the love of God, and promoting strongly their personal and reciprocal happiness. Instead of blame they deserve the highest praise. After all, the intimate life of married persons is so sacred a sphere of per-

---

15 As mentioned before, NFP must be used for serious and just reasons, not selfish ones.

sonal concern that any unwarranted intrusion is decidedly objectionable and unseemly.

It Is the Church's Business

Why, then, does the Church assume to regulate, and interfere with, the sacred intimacies of married couples? Why does she not let them and their conduct to themselves and their personal choice, direction and control? For her very dictation as to married life the Church makes herself highly obnoxious and disliked in many quarters, especially in our day. Why does she not leave this hidden and mysterious realm alone, as other churches do? Because she cannot cowardly dismiss the solemn charge of Christ that she should teach everything that He commanded. He has appointed her to be the guardian of His holy laws, and to explain them and to insist on their observance in season and out of season, regardless of the favor or disfavor of men in high or low places. Since married life is the root of all human society, every ignorance or neglect of its sacred duties is bound to be fatal. If anyone needs to be thoroughly instructed in, and opportunely advised of his or her duties, it is the married person; and the Church has been deputed by God to give this instruction and advice, and to exercise supervision over its proper and conscientious execution.

God Is the Author of the Law

It is a mistake as gross as it is widely prevalent to assume that the Church has made the law against sinful birth contraception. God is the author of this law, inherent in the very nature of man; the Church is only God's oracle declaring the law in His Name. The Church, therefore, can neither abrogate it nor mitigate it. It stands, and always will stand as it is, no matter how violently it may be assailed by the flesh and its representatives. It is therefore useless and idle to approach the priest in the confessional for the purpose of sacramental absolution if you do not intend to quit this sin once and forever, let your circumstances be what they may. Make no attempt to plead with him so he will absolve you, although you know full well and openly admit that you are going to continue your sinful practice; or even to move him to approve of your iniquitous conduct.[16] He can do neither without betraying his holy office and trust as a priest of the Most High, and without becoming an accomplice of your sin. Rather do not come to confession at all than try to tempt the minister of God to such baseness and treachery.

---

16 Sadly, some priests have devilishly misrepresented the Church's teachings on contraception, especially in the confessional. Contraception can never be justified as morally permissible.

Virginity in Marriage

The Church does not say that married couples must have children; or that they must have children in the first years of married life; or that they must have many children; or that they must have more children than they can support; or that the children must come in close succession. By no means. All that the Catholic Church teaches is that married couples, if they use the rights of marriage, must accept the consequences. But married couples need not use marriage, if they agree by mutual consent to abstain; and consequently they need not have any children at all, or have them only, please God, when they choose to live together as man and wife. The Church has numbered among her canonized saints husbands and wives who, though having every title to marital intercourse, agreed to forego it entirely and to live together in holy virginity to the end of their days. Our Blessed Mother and St. Joseph are in a class by themselves; there are others, however, who imitated their conjugal virginity, for instance, St. Casimir and his wife, and St. Elzearius and his wife St. Delphina. The Church honors them as heroes and heroines of marital continency, and proposes their example to the imitation of married couples.[17] Hence

---

17 Note: clearly this is the exception. Children are the supreme fruit of marriage. Unless a couple mutually agrees to be continent (wise to seek a priest's advice on this matter), they must remain open to children by virtue of their vows.

you need not have children, or many children, or children close together: all you need to do is to fulfill your contract with God in holy marriage, and use its rights only for the fulfilment of the purposes for which they are intended.

The Twofold Contract

When you married, you made a twofold contract: the one with your partner in marriage, by virtue of which you mutually yielded the right over your bodies to your mates: the other with God, on the strength of which you promised God solemnly and faithfully that, if He gave you the privilege of intimate married life with your partner, you would accept the consequences and the attendant responsibilities. If you did not have the intention to enter upon these terms, your marriage was null and void from the start. Now you would feel mortally hurt if your partner would not live up to the marriage contract and be unfaithful to you. Why, then, do you presume to violate your contract with God, by enjoying the privileges of matrimony, while you shirk its duties? One contract is as sacred and binding as the other. Why make so much of the one which safeguards your rights, and so little of the other which protects the rights of God?

Who Would Be Here?

If our forefathers and foremothers had practiced the sin of race-suicide[18] as many Catholic married couples are practicing it today, what would have been the result? For one thing, I should not have written, and you would not be reading, this book. Why not? Because none of us would ever have existed. I am the sixth child of my parents. You may be the first or second child: but your mother and her mother, your father and his father, all the way up the line, were they always the first or second child? We can therefore safely say that if our progenitors had used selfish and sinful family restriction, not one of us would be here today. Are you going to pay for the gift of existence by nefariously denying the boon of it to others whom God, in view of your continued use of marriage, is willing to call into being by your agency, provided you do not thwart His plans?

A Shocking Supposition

Suppose you had a daughter of about twenty years who was being courted by a young man. You suddenly became

---

18 Race-suicide refers to the gradual extinction of a certain class of people done voluntarily. Many couples have subscribed to the false notion that having more children will negatively impact the planet, or for other selfish reasons like enjoying a higher standard of living. Today, abortion is the clearest sign of race-suicide.

aware that, since there was no prospect of an early marriage after an ardent courtship, the young people agreed to practice mutual self-abuse[19] until the circumstances would warrant marriage and the procreation of offspring. Would you not be terribly incensed and cry out with utmost indignation against such shocking licentiousness and depravity? And yet upon unbiased reflection you would have to admit that after all they are as much entitled to this practice outside of matrimony as you are in it, since matrimony gives absolutely no title to it; nor does it in any way mollify its intrinsic malice. Why, then, are you not similarly shocked at your own sinful conduct?

"What Can We Do?"

"But what are we to do?" question many in utter perplexity and distress; "to have more children is out of question in our present circumstances. We cannot afford it, that's all; or the wife is in poor and delicate health, and not in a condition to be a mother again; or, even, she will be sure to die if she has to go through the ordeal of pregnancy and childbirth once more, as the doctor has positively declared. So what can we do?" Do what many other Catholic couples,

---

19 As mentioned previously by the author, self-abuse refers to masturbation and not physical abuse, though self-abuse is truly a form of spiritual abuse.

similarly, situated as you are, are doing and have been doing, with the help of God's grace, for a long time: practice self-control. That is the only virtuous birth control. If the flesh is weak, remember that God never asks the impossible, but always supplies the grace to do what He asks you to do, and that you can do all things in Him that strengthens you. If others can do it, why not you?

St. Augustine, who was no doubt as well acquainted with the weakness of human nature as any other Father of the Church, declares that unquestionably those are the happier marriages, the parties of which either live in virginity, by mutual consent, or, after having procreated children, agree to live together in virtuous continency. The union of the spirits and minds in true friendship and love is much dearer and more satisfying than the union of the bodies.

This Life's a Trial

In every state of life and profession situations arise that test human virtue to the utmost and demand heroic self-denial. These situations are not at all peculiar to married life alone, but they occur in some form or other in the celibate life in the world as well as in the life of a religious in the convent or of a priest of God. What would you think of a priest for example, who would heartily enjoy all the honors, wages and privileges attached to his office: but when there was question of performing an arduous duty, say of risking his life to administer the sacraments at the time of an epidemic, he would cravenly be found wanting? Would you not entertain the deepest contempt for so cowardly a character? Why, then, do you not similarly despise yourself for enjoying unrestrainedly the privileges of holy matrimony, while you meanly and vilely shirk its sacred duties? Does something cease to be a duty no sooner it becomes difficult?

"Forbid Them Not"

You say that, while you are perfectly willing to abstain indefinitely or forever, your partner is not; and that you have to yield in keeping with your marriage vow. Very well. But render your duty not only to man, but also to God. Be true to both, and take the consequences, whatever they will be, trusting fully in God's providence as to the ultimate result. He will provide somehow. A large number of children is quoted frequently in the Bible as a special benediction from on high. Our Lord will appreciate and reward your response to, or, at least, your acquiescence in His pleading appeal: "Suffer the little children to come unto Me, and forbid them not. For of such is the kingdom of God" (Mark 10:14). At any rate, as the good women say, it is far better to have the children on your lap than on your conscience. And particularly at your death it will be infinitely sweeter to have devoted children kneeling about your bed in loving prayer than to have specters of them haunt and torture your conscience for your horrid sins of race-suicide and selfishness.

Nature Is a Hard Creditor

Many married women are in poor health and, for that matter, many married men are, too, in consequence of the sin of prevention. They are paying nature's penalty for having outraged it. The nervous system is usually the first sufferer. The imagination and the mind are soon drawn into sympathy, and ere long health is quite generally undermined. The person grows moody, peevish, fretful, suspicious, sensitive, and despondent. The ailment is contagious and affects the other party. Sweet conjugal love, trust and harmony disappear and make room for mutual distrust, discord, and friction. Medicines will not cure this unfortunate condition if the unnatural cause of it continues. Consequently, ill health, far from being a justification for onanism, is in many instances a warning to respect nature's laws and thereby to enjoy its benefits. Reputable physicians authorize the statement that many diseases of women, cancer not excluded, would be far less prevalent if women in general in their marriage relations followed rather than transgressed nature's inviolable laws.

The Critical Case

As to the case involving serious danger of life to the woman in the face of another birth, it is dealt with best, of course, by mutual continence. It provides the husband with the best chance to display his true love for his wife in the most eloquent and substantial manner: by heroically and cheerfully denying himself, where it hurts or costs most, for the love of her. And she, in her turn, should encourage and uphold him in this resolution by checking her own connubial longings and desires accordingly. This is hard, it is true. But every profession in life imposes certain hardships and severe trials that try our mettle and test our love for God, and our worthiness to be received in His kingdom. Married life hardly has more taxing duties, not excepting the one we are discussing, than other states of life have, all things considered. We are here on earth on probation. Not by shirking difficult obligations, but by meeting them resolutely and generously, shall we gain a claim to God's recognition and reward.

Hypocrisy at Its Zenith: Folly at Its Height

The economical reason is perhaps the most universally alleged justification for sinful birth-control. It is at the same time the most flimsy and hypocritical, and nowhere more so than in our country of great and splendid opportunities for making a living. People say: "We want to give our children a good education. Education costs money. Our money will only reach for the education of one or two children. It would therefore be folly and unfair to have more." Very well. But conduct yourself accordingly, and practice virtuous abstinence while you desire no more children. No matter to what schools and colleges they send them, parents, who through sinful and selfish prevention have but one or two children, give these children the worst possible education by their own unvirtuous conduct and godless selfishness. They would do immensely better by their children, whether they have few or many, if they did their own duty to God conscientiously, and transmitted to their children this, the best element of true education, the fear of the Lord.

Large families ordinarily thrive much better economically than small families. This is accounted for naturally, because of the spirit of thrift engendered in the family and the children by their very circumstances; and supernaturally, since God always provides for those who serve Him in truth and rely upon His fatherly providence. Educationally, too, a child of a large family as a rule is better off for many reasons than the solitary child. The best education of life is in its main elements obtained in the home. At any rate, if selfish couples succeed in deceiving themselves with specious reasons, they must know that they will never deceive God, Who searches the heart and the reins. How blindly absurd the position of birth-controllers can be, was recently brought home to me by a Catholic married man, who believes in sinfully restricting his family in order, as he says, to give his children a good education. He severely blames his mother for having accepted more children than she could properly educate. Yet he himself is the seventh child of nine.

The Spread of the Cancer

What are the reasons of the spread of this moral cancer among our American Catholics? One reason is the husband's neglect of his duty to assert himself as, and actually to be the head of the wife, even as Christ is the head of the Church. The head should lead by superior intelligence and a higher sense of duty, instead of yielding in weak connivance or acquiescence when the woman feels, and winces under, the burdens of her sex and its responsibilities in married life, and directly or indirectly pleads for sinful consideration in asking her husband "to be careful" in the performance of the marriage act. From the very beginning a Catholic man should set himself firmly and finally against the very suggestion. He will be willing and glad, for good reasons, to observe continence to spare his wife; but he will never consent to any unnatural process of conjugal love. Much less will he ever himself take the initiative in intimating or insinuating so wicked a conduct. By weakly yielding to the suggestion and invitation of Eve, Adam brought a tremendous series of evils upon himself and her and all their descendants.

Love Finds a Way

The husband will ask himself, too, whether perhaps he is not indirectly the cause of his wife's disinclination to let the marriage act take its proper course. Possibly he is so strongly lacking in that tender regard, sympathetic devotion, and generous considerateness towards his wife in the period of gestation; or likely he makes so poor a living for her and the children he already has; or maybe he is all round so hard, stingy, unfeeling, cold, demanding, self-centered and self-indulgent that it is more his than his wife's fault if she recoils from undergoing all the throes and fears and dangers of motherhood to bear children to such an undeserving man. If he were what he ought to be: a Christlike man in his sentiments of love, loyalty and attachment to his spouse, she would gladly submit to her duty, however hard, for the love of him. Human nature is not mere animal nature, and it calls for a handling inspired not merely by animal passion, but by intelligent appreciation, genuine esteem and sincere love.

A High Privilege

In reality, however, man is more likely the guilty party in the sin of contraception. Maybe it was more correct to say that the guilt is about equally divided. If so, it is a sign that they both are practically ignorant of the high privilege and the inestimable distinction of parenthood. This, more than anything else, accounts for the prevalence of the detestable sin of the violation of nature in marriage. If our Catholic husbands and wives truly realized what it means to be a parent, they would never be tempted sinfully to shirk or evade their sacred responsibilities of marriage. To be a parent means to be assumed by God as an active partner in the procreation of an immortal being, made after God's own image and likeness, redeemed by the Precious Blood of His only begotten Son, and destined to shine before the throne of God in indescribable glory and blessedness throughout all the ages of eternity. But for this parent, this being would never be called into existence to give glory to God, and enjoy God, forever and ever.

An Inestimable Distinction

If in all the world there was only one couple to whom God gave the power of parenthood: how they would be envied by all others for this stupendous and almost divine privilege! All the other couples could produce marvels of human ingenuity, art and craftmanship: they could erect magnificent buildings, raise great monuments, paint wonderful pictures, carve splendid statues, compose beautiful poems or inspiring songs. Yet all of this would be as nothing when contrasted with the procreation of living, rational and immortal beings, resembling God Himself, and blending in their lineaments the features of father and mother, to transmit them unto future generations, and perhaps perpetuate them even on earth unto the end of time, as a lasting pledge of the mutual love of this fortunate couple. But why should the privilege be esteemed less merely because God multiplied it so liberally?

"Where Are the Rest?"

Do not forget this one thing: that life is a stage. You have but a brief period to play your part upon it. Soon the curtain will close, and you must give an account of your role on earth. If you then appear before the judgment seat of God with but one or two children, or even none at all, when, as you and your partner enjoyed the privileges of married life, you should have had six, eight, ten or more; and the Judge asks you sternly: "Where are the rest?"—it will not avail you to answer, saying: "Lord, I was the richest man in our town or the whole territory round about; I had the most sumptuous mansion, the finest automobiles, and the largest number of friends of the whole state; my wife's clothes, furs and jewelry were the envy of all the women of the country; I was politically powerful; we were socially prominent: in a word, we were a celebrity such as the world had seldom seen." All of this will be futile over against the cutting question of the Judge: "Where are the rest?"

No Empty Excuses

Nor will you then have the heart to advance as an excuse of your conduct the empty and futile pretexts of poverty, economical stress, disease and what not, with which you now try to ease and hush your conscience; for in the light of the omniscience of God all their hollowness and speciousness will be apparent and ghastly. All you can do then is to be silent, as was the man who had entered the festive hall without a wedding garment. And with regard to you, too, the King will say to the waiters: "Bind his hands and feet, and cast him into the exterior darkness: there shall be weeping and gnashing of teeth. For many are called, but few are chosen" (Matt. 22:13).

But if in judgment you can appear with all the children God gave you, and you can say in the words of our Lord: "Of them whom Thou hast given me, I have not lost anyone" (John 18:9);—then no matter how poor and struggling you were on earth, how delicate of body and wanting in health, how socially inconspicuous and politically obscure, the Judge will compliment you highly, and reward you amply, saying: "Well done, good and faithful servant: because thou hast been faithful over a few things, I will place thee over many things: enter thou into the joy of thy Lord" (Matt. 25:23).

Questions and Answers

The question is often asked if it is permissible for married people to agree to observe certain times and to perform the marital act only when conception seems less likely to occur. If they do the act properly when they do it, married people do not sin by restricting themselves by mutual consent to whatsoever days they choose, even if in this choice they are led mainly or exclusively by their desire not to have any more children. It is the same when, after several years of married life, to avoid an untimely increase in the family, couples consent to wait until after the woman has had her menopause, or change of life, before they resume knowledge of one another. There is nothing reprehensible in this proceeding for, while the primary purpose of marriage, the procreation of children, is not interfered with, the other objects of it are being duly pursued. But in the observance of these days or periods, married people must remember, that conception is by no means impossible. It occurs every now and then in these so-called safe seasons. Consequently the couples in question should not allow themselves to be set too firmly against having more children, so that in case they are blessed with another one, they accept it readily and with thanksgiving from the hand of God.

From what has been said it follows that it is by no means a sin for married couples, while virtuously performing the marriage duty, to harbor the wish not to have any more children, as long as they are willing to take them if they come. Nor is it unlawful for the woman to rise immediately after the nuptial act to wash herself externally for reasons of cleanliness. These things do not impede or disturb the course of nature with reference to conception. Neither is it wrong, with due resignation to God's will, to pray that there be no more children; just so nothing sinful is done to prevent their coming.

Nature's Great Mystery

The labor of childbirth for the mother remains one of the deepest mysteries of nature. Why something that is so necessary for the preservation of the human race should be coupled with so much difficulty, pain and danger baffles our understanding. The fall in paradise and the consequent curse inflicted by the Lord upon woman hardly accounts for what we call the natural mystery; for human nature, while it dropped from its preternatural and supernatural elevation through the fall, is not worse or otherwise than it would have been, had it never been elevated. Why then is childbirth naturally so arduous and perilous?

The Excellence of Motherhood

The best explanation seems to be given by the high dignity and sublime prerogative of motherhood. Nature demands a corresponding payment for whatever distinctions and privileges she bestows. She confers no higher excellence and gives no loftier station than that of motherhood: hence the big price she demands in return in the way of maternal suffering, anxiety and dread. Her reward for their endurance, however, is also in proportion to their size and intensity. Our Lord expresses it thus: "A woman, when she is in labor, hath sorrow, because her hour is come; but when she hath brought forth the child, she remembereth no more the anguish, for joy that a man is born into the world" (John 16:21).

By common consent mankind gives more consideration, appreciation and gratitude to the mother than to the father. We have a fine historical illustration of this in the rapturous exclamation of the woman regarding our Savior: "Blessed is the womb that bore Thee, and the breasts that nursed Thee" (Luke 11:27). She centered all her admiration and gave all the credit to the mother. Jesus had no father according to the flesh, of course; yet the woman was not aware of this when she declared her sentiments. The mother naturally seems also to get greater joy out of parenthood than does the father. She feels a sweeter transport and a higher pride in being able to point to her children and say with the ancient Roman matron: "Behold my jewels." In view of all this a sensible woman willingly resigns herself to the ordeal of motherhood when she feels called to it by God.

What Mankind Owes to Motherhood

It was in and through motherhood that one of our kin was elevated to the highest dignity and endowed with the sublimest sanctity any actual or possible created being is capable of—at the incarnation of the Son of God. By becoming His Mother, Mary at once and forever rose above all the angels and archangels of heaven. Through her divine motherhood she more than repaired the loss inflicted upon mankind by the first woman. For the paradise Eve deprived us of Mary gave us heaven: a prettier, a more blessed and a more glorious heaven than we should have had, had Eve never seduced Adam to sin. So much we owe to motherhood. What a grand privilege, then, accrues to every woman who becomes and is a mother after God's own heart!

Chapter VI

Sins Against Holy Marriage

Part Three

"He that hideth his sins, shall not prosper: but he that shall confess, and forsake them, shall obtain mercy" (Prov. 28:13).

Another woeful sin that is committed by married couples, but which, thank God, is not nearly so prevalent among Catholics as the one just mentioned, is adultery, or sexual disloyalty to the marriage mate. A married man has knowledge of a woman who is not his wife; or a married woman has sexual intercourse with a man who is not her husband. If the accomplice of the sin is also married, it is a case of double adultery.

A Complete Collapse

Adultery is a crime that usually involves and betrays the loss of all morale in the guilty party, and a complete collapse of every sense of honor, virtue, integrity and trust. It means that every barrier of conscience is broken, and that the victim of the adulterous passion is steering headlong towards the very bottom of moral infamy and depravity, and that, unless God checks the disastrous course by a sort of a miracle, the fatal goal will soon be reached.

The Bible gives us particularly two examples that are full of wholesome warnings and lessons for all those who are tempted to, or who are already implicated in this terrible sin, which is an act of base treachery to God, Who is the sponsor of the marriage troth, and at the same time to the one who ought to be loved next to God, to the partner in marriage, to whom the pledge of everlasting loyalty was solemnly made in the presence of God and men.

The Fatal Stroll

The first instance is that of King David. The sad story is well known. One day the king was taking a stroll on the terrace of his palace when he happened to see a beautiful woman washing herself. Instead of turning his eyes away and leading his thoughts into safe and honorable channels he arranged to meet the woman; and he sinned with her. To cover up his sin and shame he had her husband traitorously murdered. Murder likes to follow soon in the wake of adultery; at times it is the murder of the innocent party, or also of the very accomplice of the sin; then again it may be the murder of the guiltless and unhappy offspring, which is killed unborn. Anyway, there is hardly a crime from which the soul tainted with adultery seems to shrink: to such a degree does the ugly sin vitiate the conscience and annihilate every sense of responsibility.

The Wages of Sin

David's adulterous maneuvers did not remain hidden. All the shame and ignominy of them were heaped upon his head, and he had to suffer the sorry consequences of them if he lived. He portrayed for one tiling the infernal force of unholy passion. He was at that time as great and prosperous as any king on earth. He was the sweetest singer of the Lord, His most prominent prophet, and His favorite anointed one before all others. David's glory had just reached its zenith among men, and his renown and power surpassed everything Jerusalem had ever seen. In the face of all this, when the unhallowed passion was upon him, he lost all sense of appraisal, and hesitated not to sacrifice everything to its tyrannical demands: all the renown and splendor of his name; all the glory of his house; his domestic peace and happiness; the love and well-being of his wife; the good name and comfort of his children; the honor of God among men, and the good repute of religion in general: everything was forgotten and trodden under foot at the call of the vilest and meanest of thrills, the thrill of adultery. And far from being sated with this tremendous sacrifice, no sooner adultery was admitted it at once pushed its miserable victim into the abyss of black, premeditated, and cold-blooded murder. Nothing is so irresistibly swift as the course of unholy love. Before he or she becomes aware of it, its subject is deeper in crime than the unhappy person ever dreamed of being.

Resist the Beginning

When David cast that one wanton look and nursed the thoughts and imaginations it engendered, he did not suspect that within a short time he would be both an adulterer and a homicide. It would have been easy for him to resist the temptation at the very start; but once he allowed his low passions to be inflamed, resistance was out of question. From this reflection you will learn to be as cautious against danger as you must be distrustful of yourself in it. Resist manfully and decidedly at the beginning, and the sequel will create no difficulty.

This has reference to certain shows and dances of a questionable nature,[20] either because of their suggestive or

[20] This also includes any forms of entertainment or social media that are occasions of sin. A married man ought to avoid looking at the social media profiles of the opposite sex out of prurient curiosity.

lascivious character, or because of the persons or a person attending them: you will find it far easier to eschew them entirely than to try to enjoy them without harm to your marital constancy. It has reference to certain friendships with someone of the other sex other than your mate: these friendships begin, as a rule, apparently innocent and safe enough; they are mere acquaintanceships that have no further signification, and will have no other results but those of harmless converse and honorable diversion; they will be kept strictly platonic, whatever may develop. This or something similar is the initial dream of these connections. Often it does not remain a pleasant dream long, but makes room for the ghastly nightmare of ugly passion and bitter remorse over crimes the perpetration of which never entered the minds of the parties concerned at the origin of the acquaintanceship.

The Flesh Is Weak

Human nature is fickle, and the flesh is weak: hence to unleash sinful passion is like throwing a lighted match into a magazine of powerful explosives; it is impossible to foresee the volume of the catastrophe that will ensue. It is best to play safe and not to start anything that has to be stopped no sooner it grows interesting and pleasurable. Many a Catholic man, if he had observed these measures of caution and safety regarding a certain person in his employ, or a sister-in-law, or someone who belonged to the same club, or camped at the same place, or stayed at the same resort as he and his family, or whom he casually met on a train, or to whom he had some occasion to render a service in his work or profession: would today not be deploring the loss of what life contained dearest, sweetest and most precious for him, and the recovery of which is now and will ever be impossible.[21] And the same is true of many an unfortunate Catholic married woman, who dallied with a personal liking for a man not her husband, a roomer, perhaps, or agent, or casual visitor, or brother-in-law, until she suddenly found herself to be a scarlet woman of unmentionable crimes.

The King of Sinners: The King of Penitents

A further thing we notice in the conduct of King David is his seeming indifference and nonchalance after he had committed the crimes aforesaid. He showed neither worry nor concern. He went about his business and pleasures as though nothing had happened which he needed to regret. This is another evidence of the terrific power of adultery to

---

[21] Due to immodest clothing, gyms must be approached with caution. In prudence, many men have set up workout facilities in their homes.

deaden all moral sense, and to throw a pall over the conscience and still its voice. But God loved David too much as to permit him to remain long outside of His friendship and love. He sent him a monitor, a missionary or retreat-master in the person of the prophet Nathan.

And to David's eternal credit it must be said that he did not receive the grace of God in vain. He recognized and at once utilized the acceptable time, the day of his salvation. If he was great in sin, says St. Ambrose, he was even greater in penance. From the king of sinners he became the king of penitents, serving as a soothing, encouraging, and inspiring model of true conversion to all contrite sinners for all time to come, and giving them, in his penitential psalms, a wonderful lead to vent their sorrow for sin in the most loving terms before God, and thus to assuage and sweeten the bitter grief of their hearts unto heavenly solace and godlike joy and peace of mind. If you, then, have perhaps sinned after the manner of David, now that God has sent you His messenger, in the shape of this book, as a monitor, imitate David in the readiness and completeness of his penance. Then your sin, too, because of your penance, will but accrue unto your greater sanctification and glory, even as David became greater in holiness and dearer to God after his sin and penance than he had ever been before.

Adultery—Incest—Murder

Another terrible illustration of how much adultery can debauch and harden the heart of its subject is given us in the fate of King Herod of Jerusalem. He was openly and scandalously living with Herodias, the wife of his brother Philip, thus adding incest to adultery. These two crimes are not seldom together, for the adulterer does not shrink to sin with a sister-in-law, for instance, or some other close relative. St. John the Baptist charged Herod that it was not allowed for him to live with his brother's wife. Herod did not like the reprimand; but the woman, Herodias, was even more incensed by it; for a woman, when she is bad, is usually more wicked than man: as the poet says, she is a thousand steps ahead of man. So it was in this case. She swore revenge in her heart, saying she would make the prophet pay dearly for the rebuke he gave them.

Her opportunity soon came. Herod gave a festive banquet. At this banquet the lascivious daughter of Herodias gave an exhibition of an immodest dance. Herod and his guests, drunk with wine, applauded the wanton girl wildly, and Herod went so far as to promise her as her reward anything she cared to have, even if it was the half of his kingdom. Her impious mother felt that this was her chance. She bade the girl ask for the head of the prophet. Herod had not calculated on this request, and when he heard it he grew sad; but ashamed to appear a coward before his guests, he consented to the murderous petition, and commanded the head of the Precursor of our Lord to be brought in a dish and handed to the girl, who gave it to her mother, the adulteress. In the midst of a gay banquet the impious king did not recoil from unprovoked and deliberate murder on a messenger of God. He and the accomplice of his adultery gloated their eyes on the severed and bleeding head of him who dared to admonish them in their crime.

Jesus Was Silent

And it was this same Herod who not long after this event publicly mocked and ridiculed our Lord at his court, so much so that Jesus would not as much as say a single word to him. Our Lord had at least spoken to Pilate, and to the Jewish high priest who declared Him guilty of death: but He would not open His mouth to Herod. He was silent. The incestuous adulterer did not deserve another word of admonition. It would not have served him, had he got it. He was hardened in sin. If you have broken your marriage vows, but God is still speaking to your conscience, thank Him for His love and respond to it before your heart, too, is irretrievably hardened in crime, and our Lord will remain silent towards you also. There is no worse punishment can come to a sinner in this life than when our Lord, because of the sinner's hardness of heart, ceases or refuses to talk to Him or his conscience anymore.

In the first ages of the Church the sinner who committed adultery, and whose sin became public, was sentenced to do public penance for ten years. He was not permitted to enter church to attend Holy Mass or receive Holy Communion, but he had to remain outside and clothed in sackcloth and ashes, asking those who went in and came out of church to pray to God for him so he might obtain forgiveness for his dastardly crime. The nature of the sin and the justice of God have not changed since then, even if the Church has for reasons of prudence mitigated her discipline of public penance.

Stoned to Death

In the Old Testament God Himself ordained that the woman who was caught in adultery was to be publicly stoned to death; the accusing witness had to pitch the first stone at her heart, and the others were to continue pelting her with stones until she died a shameful death. In view of this attitude against adultery on the part of God, no one should let himself or herself be beguiled into what the world calls a broad or liberal mind with reference to this horrid and abominable sin against God and man.

Bismarck, the Iron Chancellor of Germany in the late nineteenth century, was not a model in many things; but in his married life he appeared to be loyal and true to his wife. In his old age he said to his wife: "God knows, that since I married you, there are only two that I loved: God and you!" Every married man should be able to say the same in all sincerity to his wife, no matter how long he lives: "Since I married you, there are only two that I loved: God and you!" And every married woman should be able to give the same assurance to her husband.

The Wedding Ring

The ring which you gave your wife at the wedding ceremony was an emblem as well as a token of your love. It was a ring of pure gold, to indicate that your love was pure and unalloyed. It was strong and round, to show the strength and the endlessness of your love for her. This is the love you professed as you put the ring on her finger; and she professed the same love for you as she accepted it. She will keep her promise if you keep yours. When she is on her deathbed, she will no doubt be able to hand you back the ring and say: "To this ring and its signification I have never been disloyal, not even in thought or desire. Since you gave it to me before the altar of God, I have loved no other man but you. You controlled all the affection and devotion of my heart, all the warmth and glow of my imagination, and all the feelings and emotions of my being. Receive this ring, then, as pure and as hallowed as it was when I received it from you on our wedding day." Happy you, if you can then respond with the same declaration of untarnished and unwavering loyalty.

The Crime of Crimes

By far the most heinous crime committed by married couples is that of abortion, by which they willfully murder an unborn child. After the woman has conceived or becomes pregnant, she consciously and deliberately has the fruit of her womb removed, either through an operation which she performs on herself, or has performed by someone else: say a doctor, midwife, or nurse; or she drinks certain teas, or takes other medicines, or uses hot baths or other appliances to recover her menses: in other words, to get rid of the child that is forming in her womb. This is murder of the worst possible kind, not only for the unnatural mother who resorts to it or allows it, but also for the husband who directly or indirectly endorses it or does not hinder it when he can; and for everyone else who somehow is accessory, or a partner, to it. And here we at times even meet with certain monstrous types of mothers and mothers-in-law who, not content with the terrible responsibility for their own personal sins, even counsel and instruct their own married daughters or daughters-in-law as to godless family restriction, not only in the way of contraception, but at times even of abortion. What a tremendous burden of sin they will have when they appear before the judgment seat of God!

If in a fit of anger you would take an ax and plunge it into the head of your little innocent child of three years and cut it in half from head to foot: this would cold-blooded murder. But in reality, it would not be so bad as the murder of an unborn child. The soul of the three-year-old child, no sooner it was separated from the body, would wing its flight to God to see Him face to face in indescribable rapture: whereas the soul of the unborn child, which is killed before it has a chance to be baptized, is forever deprived of the vision of God, due to the inhumanity of its parent, its progenitor and divinely intended angel guardian.[22]

They Cry to Heaven for Vengeance

This is in a high degree one of the sins that cry to heaven for vengeance, as much, if not more so than the sin of Cain who brutally and treacherously killed his brother

---

22 The Church's International Theological Commission (2007) offers reasons for prayerful hope that "unbaptized infants who die will be saved and enjoy the Beatific Vision."

Abel. And as Cain by his murder extinguished not only the life of Abel, but indirectly also the lives of all of those who would have descended from Abel, had he been allowed to live: so, too, abortionists are responsible not only for the loss of one human life, but also for the loss of the entire progeny of which their victim would have been the parent, had not their enormous crime interfered. And as Cain bore the ugly mark of God's anger at his sin as long as he lived and roamed aimlessly and restlessly about the world ever after, so too the abortionist is usually haunted and dogged by the specter of his murder throughout the course of his or her life.

When the daily papers record and describe some ghastly murder, many women, and men, too, for that matter, appear to be unutterably shocked; and yet they themselves in secret may have perpetrated a far more brutal homicide on their own unborn child. The Pharaoh of Egypt, who commanded that all the male infants of the Jews should be put to death by the mid wives who attended the mothers; and the cruel Herod, who had the male infants of Bethlehem and vicinity slain in his pursuit of Jesus, are historic types of unspeakable inhumanity: and yet the Jewish infants who were slain had a chance to be circumcised, and thereby go to heaven; and the Blood of Christ, in addition to their circumcision, in an especial manner availed the infants of Bethlehem unto salvation: whilst the victims of abortion have no prospect whatever of going to heaven.[23] The Chinese women, in exposing their female infants to starvation and death, make our blood run cold with horror: but these babies are often gathered by devoted Sisters or other kindly persons who baptize them and dispose their souls for the beatitude of heaven before they die: a boon that is cruelly, definitely and everlastingly denied the poor victims of abortion by their own parent, or the very one who should love them most and be most interested in their well-being for this life and the next.

Excommunicated!

Because of the heinousness of this sin, the Church punishes abortionists with excommunication from her fold, and reserves to the bishop the power to absolve them from this censure, either in person, or through a priest delegated for the purpose.

Nor does it make any difference whether abortion is committed early or late in the time of gestation: whether in the seventh or eighth month, or on the first day after conception has taken place. As soon as the mother conceives, a new human life is there. The principle of this life is the immortal soul of the child. This is evident, for if the child is permitted to develop naturally, the same identical principle

---

23 See previous footnote.

of life that was there in the beginning is with and in the child all along until it is born, and ever after. It is never replaced by any other vital principle. Everyone admits this. For if there is a substitution, when does it occur? The same soul, then, that reasons and wills in the mature man or woman, is latent with all its essence and powers in the embryo of a day or an instant. And to expel it unwarrantedly from its corporal container is nothing short of brutal murder. It belongs to God alone to separate the soul from the body of man.

Illegal Operations

Nowadays the dangers of a difficult birth are quite successfully and very morally dealt with through what is called the Caesarian operation, which saves both the mother and the child.

Other operations result in rendering conception impossible, for example the sterilization of man, or the removal of the ovaries, or some kindred process, in woman. Whenever these or similar operations are necessary because of some disease, they are lawful; but they are always immoral when they are resorted to merely to forestall further conception. If a case involving such operations occurs, it is the part of prudence to consult a conscientious Catholic physician, and to procure the advice of the priest before submitting to surgical treatment.

Whiter than Snow

It has not been a pleasant task for me by any means to mention the various sins and crimes committed directly or indirectly by married couples against the holy sacrament of matrimony; but in mentioning them as I did I have had nothing else in view than the reader's enlightenment and possible correction, and his timely recourse to God for mercy and pardon. No matter what sins you have done, and how you have done them, and how often you have done them: once you truly repent of them, and sincerely and contritely confess them, they will be forgiven by God as though they had never been. Crimson as your soul may be with sin, crime and iniquity, abortion and other murder not excepted, the Blood of Jesus, flowing upon it in the holy sacrament of penance, worthily received, will wash it clean and render it as immaculate in the sight of God as it was the moment after it was baptized, without a spot of the sins remaining. As King David, after his own terrible crimes and consequent sorrow, tells us, God washes the soul of the penitent sinner whiter than snow. There ought to be solid comfort in this assurance for every contrite sinner.

How Must You Say It?

What bothers you, however, is how to confess your sins to the priest. This ought not to be hard after the preceding instruction. You will say, for instance: Father, I have sinned by self-abuse[24] . . . by refusal of the marriage duty . . . by sinful birth control . . . by adultery with a single or married person . . . with a sister-in-law or other close relative . . . by abortion . . . so many times . . . I have not been confessing this sin for the last . . . months or years, etc., etc. Many sins can be said in a few words. There is no necessity of going into any indelicate details of the sin: just so the priest knows the nature and the number of the mortal sins, together with those circumstances that involve additional mortal sins, the confession is complete enough. If he wants further information the priest will ask for it. Do not let any false shame keep you from making a sincere and candid confession. It was a shame to sin, but it is not a shame but a great credit and honor to confess the sin with humility and contrition. Besides, do not believe that your sad story is solitary or unique in the history of the confessional. Human nature varies but little: hence you can be sure that the confessor has met your type before; in fact, he has no doubt heard far worse things than you have to tell him.

---

24 One must also confess the sin of pornography if tied to masturbation.

Take heart, therefore, and make a clean confession, and you will be at peace with God and yourself. The more you humble yourself, the higher you will rise in God's love and the higher will soar your soul's lasting joy and happiness. *But always remember our Lord's balmy yet warning words to the adulteress: "Neither will I condemn thee. Go, and now sin no more"* (John 8:11).

Chapter VII

The Education of Children

"Suffer the little children to come unto Me, and forbid them not; for of such is the kingdom of God" (Mark 10:14).

It is now time to treat of a most important duty of married couples: the education of their children. Perhaps you have no children, and have never had any. You and your wife are eager to have children, and you would welcome them with warm thanksgiving. But for some reason or other, you say, God is not hearing your fervent prayers in this regard, and your home appears more empty and incomplete from day to day. While children are a great blessing, the greatest earthly blessing, in fact, which God bestows upon married couples, still they are at the same time a great responsibility, and often prove to be a heavy cross. If God, therefore, deems it best to withhold children from you, thank Him in humble and loving resignation.

Even without children God-loving people can be perfectly satisfied and happy with each other, and they can ward off all loneliness from their home by the practice of charity and piety in an intense degree.[25]

A Grand Charity

Maybe by mutual consent you can adopt a child or two and educate them in the fear of the Lord. This is a splendid and usually a most grateful act of charity. Adoptive parents often conceive for their adopted children so strong and delightful a love that they could hardly have any greater love for their own children, or derive more gratification out of their rearing. It is God's reward for their goodness. I know that sometimes adopted children are ungrateful; but natural or carnal children are ungrateful, too; and it is not easy to say who of the two form the higher percentage in ingratitude. At any rate, if you adopt a child from good motives, the result will not affect the merit of your act in the sight of God, nor interfere with its grand reward in eternity. Jesus says invitingly: "He that shall receive one such little child in My Name, receiveth Me" (Matt. 18:5).

---

[25] Couples with infertility issues should consider NaProTECHNOLOGY, which is approved by the Church and monitors a woman's reproductive and gynecological health.

If you do not know how to go about adopting a child, go to your pastor or some other priest for information and direction. Meanwhile, keep on praying with confidence for offspring of your own. Some of the greatest saints in history, such as our Blessed Mother Mary, St. John the Baptist, the prophet Samuel of old, and several others were the reward of trustful and persevering prayers on the part of their parents who received them when already quite advanced in years. It may be remarked, too, that childlessness of couples is at times due to a certain ignorance as to the proper performance of the marriage duty, or to some physical fault which a visit to a physician may succeed in remedying.

Education: When Does It Start?

But most of you have been blessed by God with offspring. Merely to have children is not a great credit; but to bring them up carefully in the knowledge, love and service of God is a credit. To effect this abidingly, all the good sense, virtue and tact of both father and mother are required. When is the education of the child to begin? As soon as it is conceived, or, rather, at the very conception. A child that is conceived while both its parents are in proper physical and moral condition starts with a better chance for a good and fruitful life than one at whose conception its parents are not in a condition fit for generation. The nine months of gestation mean a great deal to the future life of the child. It draws the gradual formation of its body from the mother, on whose actual condition the state of the child's body very much depends. Between body and soul there is a close interrelation of influence and condition. Consequently, the condition of the expectant mother is very material to the child's fate.

The Effects of Heredity

One must not stress the burden of heredity too far: yet there seems to be ground to believe that many convicts who are in our prisons and penitentiaries today, women as well as men, would not be there had their parents been in a more favorable state at their conception and gestation. The mother, of course, plays the more important role here. She should therefore be attentive to herself in this sacred period of pregnancy. She must avoid every undue agitation and worry of mind and eschew anything smacking of excessive or passionate indulgence. This has reference not only to drunkenness or lust, but also to violent anger, jealousy, envy, revenge, and to inordinate anxiety, fear, depression, despondency, and melancholy. All these and similar sentiments, when freely pursued, are likely to affect the mind and body of the mother in a sinister manner, and to have a disastrous influence on the child that is forming under her heart.

It will benefit both mother and child if the pregnant mother keeps herself well, easy, and happy as much as possible in body and soul, and nurses feelings of the love of God and her neighbor, of trust and confidence in God's sweet providence, and of virtuous resignation to His holy will in all things. She will foster these feelings by the regular attendance at Holy Mass and by the frequent reception of the sacraments. On his part her husband will assist her towards this disposition of body and mind by behaving towards her, in the season of pregnancy, with more than ordinary love, tenderness, devotion, attachment, respect and consideration, which prompt him to anticipate her every want and to meet her most silent desires as much as his circumstances will allow.

Pregnant Mothers and Sunday Mass

As to hearing the obligatory Mass on Sundays and holydays, some pregnant mothers are exempt or dispensed early in their sacred period because of peculiar personal conditions: with the best will in the world they cannot attend Mass, for fear of nausea or some kindred indisposition. Others again keep on assisting at Mass until almost immediately before the day of their delivery. In case of doubt as to the obligation, the pastor will gladly give a dispensation, or the confessor a declaration in the matter. To discontinue going to Mass merely from embarrassment at the appearances and the consequent comment of others is hardly commendable, as a rule. It is certainly no dishonor, but rather an honor and a sign of God's favor and blessing to be a pregnant mother, and something of which a good woman has every reason to be justly proud. Of course, an innate feeling of delicacy will prompt a woman not to parade her condition unnecessarily before the world. For very good reasons God desired that the origin of human life should be veiled by a certain mysteriousness that shrinks from notice and publicity.

As the pregnancy progresses to the fifth or sixth month, the mother must be especially cautious not to exert herself unduly in a physical way. She will avoid heavy lifting, high reaching or jumping, and every other unusual tax on her bodily condition, to avoid a miscarriage. The husband will see to it that his wife is then excused from all manner of work that is likely to jeopardize her health and the life of her blessed charge.

Involuntary Miscarriage

It happens not infrequently that, without any fault at all of the parents, a miscarriage ensues. This is deplorable, of course; but it calls for nothing else than conformity to the holy will of God, Who arranges everything sweetly and wisely. In case baptism can be administered to the prematurely ejected child, it should not be neglected. The mother, taking notice of it, opens the involucrum or sack, and pours water over the contents whilst saying the words: "If you are living, I baptize you in the Name of the Father, and of the Son, and of the Holy Ghost." Life may still be there; if so, the baptism will open the gates of heaven to the child's soul. In case the administration of baptism is out of question, the soul of the child will not go to heaven, it is true; but it will neither go to a place of torments; it will go to what is called the limbo of infants, where it will enjoy natural happiness in a high degree: in a higher degree than is tasted by children or men in general on this earth. This is an opinion quite commonly held by theologians, and not at all frowned upon by the Church. At all events such a child is immensely better off in being as it is than if it had never been conceived at all: hence its parents who, as we suppose, had no guilt whatever in regard to the miscarriage, have no cause for worry or regret.[26]

---

26 Parents of an unbaptized miscarried baby have reasons to hope that their baby will be saved. According to the Catechism, God binds himself to the sacraments—He will act when the sacraments are celebrated according to the proper form, using valid matter and with the right intention—but He is God and is not bound by them. He is therefore free to bestow His grace quite apart from the sacraments as well.

"In God We Trust"

When the time for the delivery approaches, the mother will not grow over-anxious, but she will entrust herself unreservedly to the goodness and providence of God. The less timid and nervous she is, the more natural and easier will the birth prove to be. On the other hand she will be prepared against every possible eventuality, both spiritually and materially. Statistics tell us that the mortality of delivering mothers in the United States is extremely rare. The proportion is lower than it used to be, thanks to the progress of medicine and surgery; but it is still far too high, and we hope it will continue to be reduced until it is at its minimum.

All other things being equal, it is advisable to have a Catholic doctor and a Catholic midwife or nurse at the birth. Often baptism must be administered before or during the birth; and a Catholic may be counted on for doing this more reliably than a non-Catholic.

Do Not Delay Baptism

After the birth, provision should at once be made to bring the child to church for baptism as soon as possible. Any delay should be avoided by the parents. The life of a newborn infant is very precarious, and baptism is so momentous a sacrament for the child's eternal fate that no risk as to its possible loss should be taken by the parents of the child. If through their neglect the child's soul passes unbaptized into eternity, they will never get over the bitter remorse of it. In a case of necessity, when baptism has to be administered urgently, and a priest is not available, the parents should only perform the baptism when there is no other reliable person at hand to do it. Care must be taken that the water—not holy water, but ordinary clean and fresh water—be poured on the head of the infant—not merely sprinkled—while the one who pours the water says distinctly and entirely the words: "I baptize thee in the Name of the Father, and of the Son, and of the Holy Ghost." In case the child survives, it should, in due time, be taken to church so the priest can supply the other ceremonies of holy baptism. But every time baptism has been administered or only attempted at home, mention of this must be made to the priest when the child is brought to the church so the priest does not confer baptism a second time, supposing that the first administration was valid.

Reliable Sponsors

The sponsors at baptism should be chosen not merely for reasons of relationship, friendship, money, or social standing, but mainly with an eye to their good practical Catholic faith. They are to be the spiritual parents of the children, obligating themselves to attend to the Catholic education of their spiritual children in case of need, according to their circumstances. Your children may at an early date become orphans, even as other children in the same condition as yours have become orphans: they will then be fortunate if their sponsors take their sacred obligation seriously and perform it conscientiously.

In choosing names for your children always favor appropriate Christian names in preference to names that are merely odd or fanciful or cute but contain no inspiration for the bearers of them. The names of Mary and Joseph, of the apostles, martyrs, and other saints, will of themselves give the children a cue of what their parents desired them to become in the way of virtue and goodness; at the same time the very choice of such names bespeaks faith and piety in the parents.

It is the proper thing for a father to attend the baptism of his child, and thus to witness its solemn adoption as a child of God Himself. Of this high distinction and invaluable privilege bestowed upon his own offspring a Catholic man is justly proud, and he is glad to be present at the ceremony of the bestowal. It is proper, too, for the mother, at her first exit from home, to bring her child to Church, to thank God for the gift of it, and to offer it to Him in return; and on her part to be "churched", or particularly blessed by the Church. While this is not obligatory, it is highly advisable.

The Important Educational Era

Good authorities on child psychology and pedagogy have made the statement that the main part of a child's education is achieved from its birth unto its sixth year. In this period the child's mind is most observant, plastic, receptive, formative, and imitative. For this reason it is so important in the child's presence to avoid everything that might exercise a harmful influence upon it, such as cursing, swearing, abusive and immodest language, violent anger, quarreling, fighting, drunkenness and the like; and on the other hand to provide it with the best elements of discipline and training by word and especially by example. The child learns its religion and morality in the best, quickest and most lasting way by sightseeing, namely by receiving practical demonstrations of them from its parents, early and continuously. The first things it learns by heart should be the names of God, of Jesus, and Mary, the sign of the Cross, the Our Father and Hail Mary.

Beware of the Millstone

Little children are more observant than they are sometimes thought to be. Judicious parents, therefore, carefully guard against giving scandal to their children, say of three or four years even, in the performance of the nuptial rites. While the little ones may not know what it is all about at the time, the picture may linger in their minds somehow to work serious disedification in them later on when they reflect upon it. When the children get to be five or six years old, the parents must not have the boys and girls to sleep together in the same bed. This may beget in them habits of immorality that may vitiate their whole life. One of His most emphatic warnings Jesus gave in these words: "He that shall scandalize one of these little ones that believe in Me, it were better for him that a millstone should be hanged about his neck, and that he should be drowned in the depth of the sea" (Matt. 18:6).

The Catholic School

As soon as they arrive at the age of discretion, children should be given the advantage of a good Catholic education, in a parochial or other Catholic school, if possible; and they should continue to attend the Catholic school throughout their primary, secondary, and higher education as long as circumstances allow it.[27] After all, the faith and a thorough grounding in it are the best heritage Christian parents can leave their children: and they should leave them this precious inheritance at any cost. Our Catholic schools are as a rule, even in the secular branches, just as good as, and often superior to, the secular schools; hence from the viewpoint of efficiency Catholics seldom have solid grounds for refusing to send their children to the Catholic schools; and the boon of a good religious training is well worth the endurance of certain hardships, or the forfeiture of negligible and frequently questionable social advantages.

Sixteen Farms

Years ago, when I was preaching a mission in a rural district in the West, an aged and wealthy farmer was telling me of having given a farm to each of his seven children who had married. When I asked him how many children he had, he told me that he had sixteen living and two dead, all of one marriage. He obviously intended to give each of his sixteen children a farm. You will likely not be able to give each of your children a farm. But you are able to bequeath

27 Because parents are the primary educators of their children, homeschooling must be seriously considered. An orthodox Catholic school (or even a secular school when necessary) is acceptable provided the parents vigilantly oversee their children's intellectual and spiritual formation.

to everyone of your children the Catholic faith inherited from your fathers: and this is inestimably a more precious and valuable patrimony for your children than possessions of money or land, however vast. One of the best ways to transmit the true faith to your children is by giving them the privilege of a good training in a Catholic school.

Nature's Sexual Mysteries

At the age of puberty, when the girls are about thirteen and the boys about fourteen years old, certain physical developments take place in the human organism, with the nature and purposes of which it is wholesome for the children to become acquainted gradually and circumspectly. It is the part of the father to instruct his sons, and the duty of the mother to instruct her daughters regarding the origin, the meaning, and the reproduction of life. It is far better that the children obtain this valuable and necessary information from wise parents in a decent and sacred manner, than that they get it in a vicious and objectionable way from tainted and corrupt companions. This instruction properly given will serve the children as a safeguard and protection in the dangerous years of adolescence. When the angel informed our Blessed Mother that she was to be the Mother of God, she replied: "How shall this be done, because I know not man?" (Luke 1:34). Evidently, though she was but about sixteen years old at the time, she had a knowledge of the sacred process of human generation; and yet she was the purest of the pure, and more innocent than any angel of God.

Little Crosses: Big Crosses

Little children are said to be little crosses, while big children are said to be big crosses. Formerly it used to be said that little children step on the mother's dress, while big children step on their mother's heart. Woman's dress today renders this proverb out of date, but the nature of children is the same as ever. Whatever those sayings may mean, parents make a big mistake in believing that their growing or adolescent children need their attention and correction less than before. They often need them more, although perhaps in a different way. To achieve the best results in educating their children in the fear of the Lord, it is above all necessary that father and mother work harmoniously and mutually supplementarily. In other words, they work together hand in hand, upholding and endorsing one another, and the one supplies what the other lacks. The mother will usually abound in grace, tenderness, sympathy, gentleness, and kindness: the father will represent dignity, power, firmness, authority, and discipline. As marriage in general, the burden of education will be carried like a yoke. If both go into the same direction, aim at the same goal, and keep about the same tempo, the burden becomes easy, light, and agreeable: whereas if one insists on going one way, and the other is stubborn about going into the opposite direction, there will be nothing but confusion, failure, disappointment, and ruin. For the sake of harmony, then, in this very important department of family life, wise concessions from both parties are much in order, and worth all they cost.

The Deadly Lake Ride

A story is told about the evil consequences of division or disharmony of parents in the upbringing of their children. A girl had asked permission of her father to take a ride in a boat on the lake. It was Sunday afternoon. The father refused permission. He would not accede to the request, no matter how much his daughter pleaded. When he left the house for a walk, the girl entreated her mother to allow her to take the ride. The mother yielded but cautioned the child not to let her father suspect that she granted her the permission. Several hours later a storm suddenly swept over the lake and surrounding territory. The father, who had returned home, was just telling his wife how much he was congratulating himself for not allowing his daughter to go on the lake when a messenger knocked at the door to bring the sad news that the boat containing the girl and her companions was upset in the storm and that all its passengers were drowned. He added that the corpse of the girl had been recovered and was ready to be brought in by the men who were waiting outside. Imagine the consternation of the father, and the guilty and crushed feeling of the mother. Such a catastrophe may not happen often in the physical order, but morally it is, alas, but too frequent.

The Shipwreck of the Soul

Many Catholic children suffer moral and religious shipwreck due to a lack of union and cooperation of father and mother in their education. And what has been said regarding the parents in their relation to one another in this matter ought to comprise the teachers and pastors of their children also, in the sense that parents should cooperate all they can with them, too, in promoting the welfare of their children. They will consequently defend and support the authority of pastors and teachers in all things, and never permit the children to make faultfinding or otherwise derogatory remarks about them; much less will they ever openly take a child's part against the teacher or pastor. No one is faultless. Teachers and pastors make mistakes as do other human agents. But it damages rather than benefits the children if their parents tolerate, or even endorse a critical, carping, disparaging and rebellious attitude on their part towards teachers and priests.

The Power of Love

The best, the most agreeable and effective way for parents to achieve fine results in rearing their children is by harboring for them, and plainly exhibiting towards them genuine, consistent, impartial, generous, sympathetic, and unselfish love. Love begets and elicits counter-love. It is easy for you to guide and train a child that sincerely and fondly loves you. Be a real companion to your children; enter into their interests, take part in their games and pastimes, as much as possible, and help them with their studies and other laudable efforts towards success. You will thus win their trust and confidence. They will tell you their secrets, acquaint you with their ambitions, and inform you of their friendships and their loves. They will appreciate your counsels and welcome your guidance. It will be easy for you then to know the company they keep, the amusements they frequent, and the acquaintances they make. In other words, parental watchfulness, instead of being an irksome task, will be for you an agreeable duty.

Lifeless Idols

There are parents who in regard to their children are very delinquent in the necessary vigilance. They are like the idols mentioned in the Bible: "They have mouths and speak not;

they have eyes and see not; they have ears and hear not; they have noses and smell not; they have hands and feel not; they have feet and walk not" (Ps. 113:5, 6, 7). Their children practically do as they please, without opposition or hindrance of their parents. They go where and with whom they like. They stay out as long as they choose. They read whatever they fancy. When they become involved in some scandal, say the son or daughter becomes an unwedded father or mother, the parents throw up their hands in horror. They grow terribly indignant and exclaim that they cannot understand why such a disgrace should ever have befallen their family. But often they are more guilty than the child. They were mature in years and had the experience of life; had they watched properly and prudently over their children, their going and coming, and had they used kindness and firmness upon them according to their needs, the lapse would likely have been avoided. After it has taken place it is too late to become indignant. When the girl is in dire distress, and faces ostracism and disdain on the part of the cold and cruel world, and that from many apparently respectable people who in their private lives may be immensely worse than she has been, it is not the time for her parents to increase her mental tortures by apathy and severity, and thus perhaps to drive her to a worse crime than her first offense, namely to abortion and, possibly, suicide: but then it is the part of sensible and conscientious parents to take her back to their hearts in warm and generous sympathy, forgiveness and love, and to provide her in her delicate condition every protection and assistance.

The Black Sheep

Of course, if without any recourse to sinful practices the matter can be kept secret, it must be done for the girl's and the family's sake. If it cannot be concealed, the girl and the family should bear the consequent disgrace with humble patience and resignation to God's providence, and in the spirit of compunction, and atonement for sin. There are many worse sins done in public and in private, which the world does not visit with its scorn and excommunication, but which are nevertheless grosser and more damnable in the sight of God.

While the parents are often as much or more at fault than the child that goes wrong, it must yet be admitted that sometimes the best parents, despite all their good efforts in the interest of their children's education, are afflicted with a wayward child that brings shame upon the family and overwhelms the hearts of the parents with bitterness. This is one of the mysteries of the inscrutable providence of God, which it is given us devotedly to adore, but never to fathom in this life. Still, it is good for all parents to remember that eternal vigilance is the price they are asked to pay for the welfare and felicity of their children. In addition to this it is consoling for good parents of bad children to reflect that, even as the winter wheat that is covered with snow seems hopelessly dead and gone, but soon comes to view again under the sun's glow, so, too, a boy or a girl that has grown bad, and appears to be desperately lost to virtue and to God, is suddenly touched by God's grace and the warmth of the parents' love, and rises and thrives again unto goodness and holiness of life.

The Important Choice

The point of the choice of their state of life, or of their vocation, on the part of their children must be of great concern to parents, and should always enlist their keen interest, sympathetic guidance, and substantial help. While the children are and should remain free in the choice of a vocation, the counsel and advice of the parents can be of great assistance to them. But the parents must not grow dictatorial and narrow in the matter, nor allow themselves to be swayed by some blind prejudice or selfish leaning. Their exclusive aim must be the child's own best interests.

Perhaps your sons or daughters want to consecrate themselves to God in the priesthood or the Religious life. If they exhibit any such tendencies, foster and nurse them prudently and fondly, thanking God for this great grace all the while. God can hardly confer a greater distinction upon a family than by calling one or more of its children to His exclusive service, either in His sanctuary as priests and ministers of the divine mysteries, or as friars, brothers, monks, or nuns to pursue His works of religion, education, and charity. The opinion has been expressed—although it has never been authoritatively endorsed by the Church—that if a family gives a child to God in the way just mentioned, the entire family goes to heaven.

The Lord Is Generous

It would be imprudent to stress this mere opinion too far, but the gospel tells us that some of the relatives of the apostles got to be very close to our Savior; and they were no doubt drawn to Him through the apostles. The Lord is as generous today as He was then. And the faith has been preserved in many a Catholic family, and in every member of it, mainly through the consecration of one of the children to God's special service. Hard as it may be for parents to surrender a child to God in this manner—He usually asks the best one—the pain of separation will be compensated for, not only by an eternal reward, but also by a hundredfold reward in this life, in the shape of the many joys and consolations coming to them directly or indirectly from this child. From none of their children who remain with them and get married by and by, do they ordinarily derive the same comfort, even on earth. God is good to those who love Him. Whereas, if parents thwart the high designs of a priestly or Religious vocation which God has upon their children, they may seriously incur His displeasure, and because of the various misfortunes resulting to them and their children, they may live bitterly to rue their selfishness and stubbornness. On the other hand, no prudent parent will attempt to influence a child unduly to become a priest or Religious if there be no true calling. This would be exposing the child to the risk of serious unhappiness and spiritual disaster.

The Bane of Mixed Marriages

If your children choose the married state, your advice and direction can be of great benefit to them in the choice of a proper mate. Silent and diplomatic guidance may often be more effective here than open direction. Love is a jealous factor and resents being controlled by outside influences from whatsoever source. Catholic parents will above all do what they can to have their children to marry in the faith: in other words, to shun mixed marriages. Some mixed marriages terminate favorably all round, it is true; but as a rule—statistics say nine times out of ten[28]—mixed mar-

28 Rite of Christian Initiation (RCIA) is a possible solution for bringing the non-Catholic spouse into the faith.

riages develop most perniciously for the Catholic party and its offspring. Consequently, on the face of it the risk is too great to be considered or tolerated by parents who have the real welfare of their children at heart.

From the very beginning, therefore, they let their children know and feel that they are resolutely, irrevocably, and inexorably set against mixed marriages on their part in any and every form; not at all from a spirit of narrowness or bigotry—for they readily admit that non-Catholics are often very fine and good men and women—but from a spirit of common-sense interest in the future welfare of their offspring. No matter how and from what angle we consider a mixed marriage, from its very nature it starts out with a serious disagreement of elementary views and principles of life between the contracting parties; and, what perhaps ought to weigh heavier in the balance of sound judgment, it is in reality a most unequal bargain, with all the inequality in disfavor of the Catholic party: the Catholic binding himself or herself for life—"until death do us part"—while the non-Catholic mate practically assumes the pledge of fidelity only as long as it will in the sequel be found to be acceptable. No sensible person would agree to a similar contract in any other affair of life however little was involved: why, then, should it be considered in the most important concern of life? If man and woman need a life's helpmate in any department, it is in the practice of the true faith, in which they require all the efficient encouragement and stimulation by word and example which they can possibly get. If instead of a helpmate in their religious profession, they procure what is virtually and at best a handicap and a brake to whatever spirit of faith they may possess, they are aiding neither their own chances for eternal salvation, nor the chances of those who may spring from their marriage. Life is real, and eternity is long.

Why the Difference?

While parents cannot altogether control the nuptial bents of their children, the parental influence, when discreetly and seasonably employed, will go far in forestalling mistakes. In some Catholic families every child marries a non-Catholic, while in the same place and under the same social and other conditions there are other Catholic families every child of which makes a good Catholic match. What usually accounts for the difference? The attitude of the parents.

In the first instance, there is reason to fear, the parents either have not enough faith or conscientiousness to care whether their children marry Catholics or not; or if they care, they have not enough good sense, judgment, and tact to win the confidence and love of their children beforehand, and thus to steer them clear of these dangerous alliances. In the other case the parents are the friends and companions of their children. They make home so pleasant for them that the children prefer to be there rather than anywhere else outside of church. They take part in everything that interests and amuses their children. They allow the children to bring their friends to their home and, provided they are unexceptionable, they show them a warm welcome and a generous hospitality. They have various home parties: birthday parties, surprise parties, and the like, to which they have the children to invite their Catholic young friends of both sexes, and they themselves take part in the music, dances, songs, and other accessories of the feast. Sometimes certain friendships spring up between their children and the young people who frequent their home; and the friendships gradually ripen into love, courtship and marriage to the satisfaction and happiness of all concerned.

Mean Parents

Parents who, from a selfish love of ease and comfort, or even from a motive of egotistical jealousy, which prompts them to keep their children for themselves rather than surrender them to another, forbid their home to the friends or company of their children either directly or indirectly, by treating them coldly and rudely, have much to answer for if the children strike out for themselves, and in impatient self-assertion meet their friends stealthily, and contract obnoxious alliances in or out of marriage. The children have a right to a reasonable share of the parental home and its amenities, and autocratically to deprive them of the use of this right, suggests neither piety, charity nor justice on the part of their unfeeling and inhuman parents.

Wise Parents

Wise parents exercise a tactful, considerate, yet close vigilance over their children in the period of courtship. While they may be convinced that their sons and daughters are trustworthy, they will yet remember that they are made of flesh and blood; that they are young and inexperienced; that they have more sentiment than good sense; and that they are often unaware of the catastrophe resulting from unrestrained love. The parents will therefore act as sympathetic guides and moderators of their children who are in love. They will not allow their courting to become passionate. For this reason, they will not allow the visits to be too frequent, nor to be prolonged too far into the night, nor to be carried on without due protection and supervision. If there is to be any excess here, it will preferably be on the side of severity rather than indulgence; this will safeguard the wellbeing of the lovers more: although the golden mean, as in all other things, is the best here, too. The more the company keeping can be done in the family circle, the better for all involved. Sometimes, of course, the young people want to be alone to exchange sentiments that are too sacred for the ears of others. But as a rule, the less they are alone before marriage, the more and the longer they will likely enjoy being alone after marriage.

The Lethal Engine

Here a word may be in order regarding the automobile and its use by young people. A secular judge of considerable prominence has expressed it as his conviction that the automobile is a stronger and a more baneful factor of immorality than the bar in its worst days ever was. The bar could not be frequented by girls whose reputation still meant something to them: whereas the automobile carries a certain air of respectability which, alas, is in many cases but the merest veneer of the grossest depravity, yet which is sufficient justification for girls of the best families to entrust to it their innocence, virtue and reputation, often to have them all ruined, and their happiness blasted for life, through a single ride.[29] Parents should be vigilant regarding the rides their children take, and how, with whom, when

[29] It is advised that young people socialize in a group setting or in public spaces.

and where they take them. A prudent chaperonage is their best protection, physically as well as morally.

Obedience Ceases: Love Goes On

When children marry, they establish a household of their own, and are automatically withdrawn from parental authority. Yet, if a married child no longer owes obedience to its parents, the duty of exhibiting love, reverence, gratitude, and devotion to parents never ceases. It is a matter of sad observation that children, who before their marriage were invariably dutiful, loving, and attentive to their parents, after their marriage often grow very selfish, hard, and cruel towards their parents or parents-in-law. They turn against them somehow, and refuse them the ordinary marks of Christian charity, let alone the tokens of filial respect, gratitude, and homage. For this there is never any excuse, and it will be visited by God in His own way and manner sooner or later; and usually the punishment is meted out after the manner of the sin; these ungrateful children will before long feel the sting of ingratitude and indifference from their own offspring.

Jealous Parents

On the other hand parents sin, too, when they mar, and sometimes ruin entirely the happiness of their married children by their jealous, selfish, and meddlesome manner. They poison and turn the minds of their children against their mates by certain slurs, insinuations, and accusations of a vile nature, inspired by a vicious motive. These parents lose sight of the words of the Bible: "Wherefore a man shall leave father and mother, and shall cleave to his wife" (Gen. 2:24). According to this inspired utterance a married child belongs more to its mate than to its parents; and every parental conduct that aims to disturb or overthrow this divine arrangement is godless and reprehensible. The parents embitter their own lives by it every time.

It is usually advisable for married children to live apart from the parents and relatives of both sides. This will help to prevent a serious rupture that may have the saddest consequences. Amicable and agreeable relations can and ought to be maintained to the benefit and pleasure of all parties concerned. This maintenance is easier at a certain distance, when visits will not be too frequent, and uncalled-for interference in one another's business not so tempting. Instead of that there will likely be a sound love for one another, a desire, and an eagerness for one another's company, together with a great deal of mutual sympathy, helpful counsel, and valuable assistance in case of need. Mothers-in-laws often bear the brunt of many jokes. Yet most mothers-in-law are good and sensible women, who know their place and keep it, who are sincerely loved by their children-in-law as well as by their own children as long as they live, and whose departure from this life is keenly felt and bitterly deplored by both, in consequence of their truly motherly love, unselfish solicitude, and tactful prudence.

Give and Take

Not infrequently parents have to live with their married children or vice versa. Here, too, if both parties have and exercise good sense and unselfish love, conditions can be made not only tolerable but quite agreeable and sweet. This will be effected best if both parties carry out the injunction of the Apostle: "Bear ye one another's burdens; and so you shall fulfill the law of Christ" (Gal. 6:2). Old people have different views, tastes and sentiments than young people. If both insist on the prevalence of their own views, there can be no harmonious and happy life. But if both are ready to make allowance for the views of the other party, there will be much room for the practice of genuine virtue as well as for the enjoyment of substantial peace. If the one is more ready to yield to the other than to force his own pleasure, there will be much mutual good-will and consequent bliss.

But concessions should be equally apportioned, and not always made by the same party and enjoyed by the other. Both will then derive the benefit from this arrangement in the exchange of reciprocal help: their pains will be divided and diminished, while their joys will be shared and multiplied.

Young people must particularly remember that old age has its infirmities of the mind and also the body. Not without reason is it called the second childhood. But while the elderly usually disclose the troublesomeness, fretfulness, and vexatiousness of children in a reinforced degree, they never offer the cuteness, the dearness and affectionateness of children in compensation. The bearing with them patiently requires considerable virtue and self-control. Yet no conduct will please God more and call for a higher reward in this life and in the next, so it is cheerfully and consistently rendered: whereas rudeness, coldness, and hardness to aging parents prepare a very hard way for the offender. On their part, the elderly should try to ward off the mental and temperamental weaknesses of age as much and as long as possible by maintaining an optimistic and cheerful outlook upon life in general and their own in particular; by keeping themselves from getting oversensitive, suspicious, and jealous; by eschewing all imaginations of being ill-treated, considered in the way and a burden, and desired off the stage of life by the younger element. These and similar thoughts are often the merest fictions of a morbid or aging mind and have no foundation whatever in the facts of the case. As a rule, elderly parents are very welcome, as long as they themselves do not become strangers to virtue and good sense.

Ruth and Noemi

What wonderful and helpful companions mothers and mothers-in-law can be to their married daughters and daughters-in-law; and what a great blessing is attached by God to the piety and love exhibited to these mothers by their respective daughters—and the same holds good relatively to the male sex, of course—illustrated clearly by the story of Ruth in the Bible.

When Ruth's husband died, her widowed mother-in-law Noemi suggested to her to return to her own kin, among whom she would feel more at home. Ruth answered: "Be not against me, to desire that I should leave thee and depart: for whithersoever thou shalt go, I will go: and where thou shalt dwell, I also will dwell. Thy people shall be my people, and thy God my God. The land that shall receive thee dying, in the same will I die; and there will I be buried. The Lord do so and so to me, and add more also, if aught but death part me and thee" (Ruth 1:16, 17).

As a result of this filial attachment and Noemi's response to it, Ruth, with the aid and guidance of her mother-in-law, became one of the foremothers of the Messiah. Orpha, on the contrary, who was another daughter-in-law of Noemi, and who had lost her husband about the same time as Ruth, but who parted company with her mother-in-law after giving her a farewell kiss, was never heard of again. There is much wholesome solace in this episode for those married men and women who observe the fourth commandment after their marriage; and a salutary caution for those who ignore it by shirking their sacred duty to their parents, and by unfairly leaving their whole support and care to one of their more conscientious brothers or sisters. "Honor thy father and thy mother, that thou mayest be long lived upon the land which the Lord thy God will give thee" (Exod. 20:12).

Chapter VIII

Husband and Wife

"Let everyone of you in particular love his wife as himself: and let the wife fear her husband" (Eph. 5:33).

A word remains to be said concerning the relations between man and wife in general. They cannot be depicted in a nice and more appealing manner than in the words of St. Paul which are read in the epistle of the nuptial Mass: "The husband is the head of the wife, as Christ is the head of the Church. . . . Therefore as the Church is subject to Christ, so also let their wives be to their husbands in all things. Husbands, love your wives, as Christ also loved the Church, and delivered Himself up for it. . . . So also ought men to love their wives as their own bodies. He that loveth his wife, loveth himself. For no man ever hated his own flesh; but nourisheth and cherisheth it, as also Christ doth the Church" (Eph. 5:23 sqq.). In sacred intimacy and in sweet, blissful, and prolific love no union has equaled that of Christ and His Church. The apostle desires married people should copy this union and its happiness in their conjugal life. They will do this by imitating Christ and His Church, respectively.

The Grandest Love

"Husbands, love your wives, as Christ also loved the Church." Christ loved and loves but one Church. He concentrates upon her exclusively. Whatever He thinks, plans or schemes; whatever He says, does and ordains; whatever He bears, suffers, and endures: it is all for His one Church. All His love, affection, devotion, and consecration are focused on her. Not once has His love wavered, faltered, or hesitated. Not once was it ever tempted to consider strange charms or measure foreign lures. There have been many rivals of the Church for the patronage and love of Christ; many went so far as to assume His Name and go under His pretended protection: but they never received His attention or attachment for a single moment, and they went to naught in consequence. He knew and recognized and loved but one Church, and He was unapproachable to, and intolerant of, any and every one of her competitors for His love.

Similarly, a good Catholic husband will love his wife. He will devote himself to her, exclusively of every other woman, with his whole heart, and his whole soul, and his whole mind, and with all his strength. She will possess all his love and his entire affection. Whatever he thinks or says, plans or desires, promotes, or executes: everything aims to please his wife, and to render her existence happy and sweet. In this concentration he never weakens, nor is he ever distracted from it by any strange feminine charms or seductive fascinations. He gives these no chance to function in his regard, because of his being altogether and irrevocably riveted to the wife of his bosom, his heaven-given mate, companion, sweetheart, and friend.

True Love Never Dies

The love of Christ for His Church was and is peacefully constant and lasting. He loved the Church not only in the beginning, when she was a novelty, and when she was fresh, interesting and charming with youthful enthusiasm for, and heroic devotion to, Him: but He loved her just the same later on when she began to show evidence of the weaknesses of the human element within her; when her members became disunited and often grew variously tainted and contaminated with sin and vice: then, too, He abided with her in unfailing love, unswerving attachment and saving protection. He loves His Church today, over thousand years after His mystic espousals with her, as much as He ever loved her, without the least diminution of ardor or deflection of love.

In like manner a good Catholic man loves his wife not only in the first period of marriage, when she is young, beautiful, sprightly, vivacious and generally charming, and when their union still has the spice of novelty and freshness: but he will love her as much or even more as years wear on, and when she begins to discover the weaknesses of her sex and the foibles of her character, which he perhaps never suspected, and by the extent of which he is considerably surprised and, in a way, disappointed. Yet this disappointment in no way affects or decreases his love for her: on the contrary, if anything, her very faults and shortcomings bring out his love in its best, most unselfish, and heroic manifestations. This is particularly verified when his wife suffers a serious illness or some similar misfortune. Her weakness or adversity becomes the triumph of his love, even as our Lord's love for His Church showed to best advantage in the times of her trials and persecutions.

Love Is Operative

Christ loved His Church with a real, actual, and practical love. His love did not merely consist of sweet phrases, endearing terms, and glowing professions of love; but it showed itself in His entire conduct, and by His deeds. Whatever He undertook or performed: His preaching, His miracles, His example of holiness, His endowing the apostles with power from on high, His death on the Cross, His resurrection, His ascension, His sending of the Holy Spirit: everything was a substantial rendition of love for His Church. And throughout the ages His active assistance and protection of her never cease or lessen in force and effectiveness.

So, too, must be a good Catholic man's love for his wife. While he will not fail to give her repeatedly, with loving prudence, the tender professions of attachment and devotion a woman naturally craves and enjoys from the object of her love: he will be careful to back up these professions with continuous exhibitions of real service and practical sacrifice inspired by his love for his wife. All his labors and toils, all his endurance and patience, all his plans and designs, in his work, trade, profession or business aim to please her, and to render her life discreetly easy, comfortable, and enjoyable. Just so she is happy he does not mind how much he must work, sweat, suffer, and endure: even as Christ shrank from no labor or sacrifice in the interest of His Church.

This is the ideal relation of a husband towards his wife. Perfection is seldom, if ever, realized by mere men on this earth. Consequently men are also known to sin variously against this ideal of marriage. Yet it must be owned to their credit that by far many Catholic husbands strive earnestly to meet the full requirements made upon them, and this with a considerable amount of success, all allowance being made for the native infirmity of human nature. Some husbands, however, fall pitiably short of the ideal through their own fault.

The False Husband

Here we meet first the disloyal husband. Not content with the one wife, to whom in the presence of God, angels, and men, he solemnly swore exclusive and undying love and attachment, he goes after strange and adulterous loves, usually to the ruination of his own and his wife's happiness. For a vicious and short lived sensuous gratification he is willing to jeopardize and forfeit the sweetest and most precious thing this life contains for an honorable man: the abiding trust and encompassing love of a good woman. He is like a man who prefers a deadly drug to wholesome food: with similar results as to his life's happiness and peace. "The deceitful man shall not find gain: but the substance of a just man shall be precious gold. In the path of justice is life: but the by-way leadeth to death" (Prov. 12:27, 28).

The Alcoholic and Gambler

There are other married men who wreck the happiness of their married life through brutish selfishness which usually takes the form of alcoholism. Nothing must come in the way of their beastly self-indulgence. All considerations for the welfare, peace and comfort of the wife are mercilessly and ruthlessly sacrificed to it. The well-known story of the alcoholic's dream illustrates the havoc this terrible vice plays with what married life holds dearest and best. A man given to drink related at the breakfast table one morning that he had had a bad dream during the night. He saw four rats. One was very fat and bloated; another was blind; while the remaining two were very lean and weak. He wondered what a dream like that could mean. His little son of twelve years, who was seated at the breakfast table with his mother and father, said naively: "Papa, that's easy. I know what that dream means. The big fat rat is the bootlegger from whom you buy your booze. Mama and I are the lean and weak rats, for we have hardly enough to eat to keep us alive. The blind rat is yourself, for if you were not blind to your well-being and ours, you would never drink as you do." Here, too, in every case, "the wages of sin is death" (Rom. 6:23).

What is true of alcoholism applies with proportionate force to the vice of passionate gambling, which sometimes suddenly, and as a rule ultimately, involves the most promising and the sweetest marital unions in catastrophe and disgrace.

The Selfish Husband

Finally some married men, although not given to adultery, drink, or gambling, fail miserably as husbands because of a violent and uncontrollable temper, which inclines them to be rude and very abusive to their wives at times; or because of a temperamental coldness and indifference, by reason of which they are self-centered and self-satisfied; they show no sympathy for, or interest in, the wife's conditions, occupations, needs and desires; they either do not reflect that she is of a different sex, and may be of a different temperament than they, or they do not care if she is or not; they are not going to put themselves out a particle to please her, or even to meet her half way towards a mutual understanding and a tolerable living relation. They want to be left alone, and they despise anything smacking of emotionalism or sentimentality in their married life. All they desire in the way of marriage is to use the wife to satisfy their sexual passion when they feel an inclination for it; but she must never expect that they are ever going to exhibit her any tenderness, affection, or endearment, flowing from a personal love or regard for her. All of this is beneath them, and the mere thought of it disgusts them. They are selfishness incarnated, and do not deserve the name of husband.[30] Their conduct is the very antithesis of the injunction of St. Paul: "So also ought men to love their wives as their own bodies. . . . For no man ever hated his own flesh; but nourisheth and cherisheth it, as also Christ doth the Church" (Eph. 5:28, 29). If the wife, rebelling against so unfair and mean a treatment, reciprocates by leaving such a husband severely alone, and by divesting herself of all concern about his person and affairs, he is merely getting what he deserves.

The Miser Husband

To this class must be added the miserly husbands, who treat their wives, as far as the economy of the house is concerned, as mere domestics or, rather, as slaves. They give them barely enough money to conduct the household decently, and even this money the wives must beg and plead for with great humiliation and confusion. No domestic would put up with such a situation; but since the wife is bound by her sacred marriage vows, these unfeeling husbands abuse her and degrade her to a condition of servitude. On the

---

[30] This would also include those husbands who are married to their work and not their spouse, who put their family and friends before their spouse. They would rather play golf and watch sports than spend quality time with their spouse.

outside they may make a show of generosity and magnanimity, merely to be the more tyrannical and stingier to the one who has the strongest claim upon their attention and liberality. Far from being mature men, these tyrants are the meanest and vilest of slave-drivers. In consequence of their miserliness they never know the sweetest experience of a married man: the spontaneous and wholehearted love, respect, and admiration of a good and devoted woman.

Honey versus Vinegar

It is as far removed as it can be from the Christian conception to consider the wife as a mere property that can be dealt with at the caprice and whim of the husband. She is a co-partner in the marriage contract, entitled to equal rights and privileges as the husband. By attending to her duties as wife and mother she has a claim to a respectable and becoming living, not of a slave or even of a child, but of a coordinate partner of the matrimonial firm. She should therefore be given as liberal an allowance for the household as the income of the family permits, and she should be at liberty to dispose of it according to her own discretion without any duty of accounting for expenditures, and more still, without any sleuthing, bickering or faultfinding on the part of her husband. The more margin is allowed the wife in the management of the house, the better is it likely to be handled. According to St. Francis de Sales more flies are caught with one drop of honey than with a barrel of vinegar; similarly much more is achieved by an ounce of love than by a ton of rudeness and boorishness. This is particularly applicable to the relation of marriage in which love is or at least ought to be more at home and in its peculiar domain and power than anywhere else in life.

The Church Loves Christ

"As the Church is subject to Christ, so also let the wives be to their husbands in all things." The Church loves Christ exclusively. Her one aim is the spread of His kingdom, the conquest of immortal souls for Him, the achievement of His glory, and the supreme dominion of His love. No rival for her love is ever considered, and every competitor for her attention is hopelessly disappointed. There have been ever so many false prophets who tried every open and furtive deceit to wean her away from her divine Spouse, but never for a moment did she waver or even deign to attend to their advances. She was consecrated to Christ, entirely and unreservedly from the start, and to this consecration she is true with abiding loyalty and heroic persistency, in bad times as well as good times, in the period of adversity as well as in the heyday of prosperity. Her devotion and attachment to Christ never change or wane. Like Christ Himself, they are always the same: the same today as they were over two thousand years ago, and as they will be at the end of time.

In this way, says St. Paul, should a woman be loyal and true to her husband. He must be the one and only object of her love. He engages all her heart's tenderness and affection. He controls all the thoughts of her mind, and all the dreams of her imagination. Aside of him no rival whatsoever, let him be ever so charming and bewitching, has any chance to be observed or considered by her, let alone to be encouraged or accepted. Her one passion in life is concentration on the husband of her bosom. From this she derives her best joys and her sweetest thrills. She would not exchange him for any man in the world, for in her eyes he is the noblest, grandest, and dearest specimen of Christian manhood there is. Anyway, if there is a better one, she does not want to know of it. In this appreciation and love of her husband she increases rather than decreases as the years roll on, and the end of their lives finds her as devoted, loyal, and attached to her mate as she was on her wedding day.

The Church Trusts Christ

The Church has always had full confidence and absolute trust in Christ and His fidelity. She was never suspicious or jealous of Him. At times it almost seemed as though He was neglecting His fidelity to her. In the bloody persecutions that threatened her with extinction she had to take refuge under the earth to be safe from her cruel enemies. She might have asked: "Where is my divine Spouse? Why does He not hurry to my defense? Why does He suffer me to be reduced to such a pass? Has He forgotten me? Is He going after a strange love, after another church that is to replace me?" Not once did the Church harbor the least suspicion of His loyalty. All appearances to the contrary notwithstanding, she was always sure and restful in her trust in Him, in His timely help and abiding protection.

This is the manner of confidence a Catholic woman places in her husband. She is not only convinced of his unwavering fidelity to her, but she lets him know and feel that it is not in her power ever to doubt or question his conjugal loyalty. From the beginning, therefore, of her married life she consistently rejects every temptation to suspiciousness and every inclination to jealousy. She fights shy of all those insidious female whisperers, whether they pose as well-meaning relatives, disinterested friends, or solicitous neighbors or acquaintances, who try to poison her marital happiness by the venom of malicious gossip or slanderous insinuations implicating her husband. The source of these hypocritical confidential advices is usually nothing else but base jealousy, that is stung by the sight of the nuptial bliss of others and goes out ruthlessly to disturb or destroy it. Much more is a good woman on her guard not even by way of a joke to make a remark to her husband, or to cast a slur or aspersion intimating that perhaps he is not so true as he pretends or ought to be. One such ill-advised joke has often demolished the sweetest connubial love forever.

The Church Works and Suffers for Christ

The love of the Church for Christ is not only theoretical and sentimental, but it is active and practical. The Church works and suffers for Christ, cheerfully and continuously, the more the gladder. Whatever she does: if she baptizes children, absolves sinners, invites communicants to the Holy Altar, clothes nuns, ordains priests, consecrates bishops, crowns popes, builds churches, schools, seminaries, colleges, orphanages, hospitals, and the like, sends missionaries abroad in the land or into foreign countries: it is all and exclusively for Christ. She does not seek her glory, but that of Christ. His joy is her joy, His victory is her victory, His triumph is her triumph.

In like manner a good woman's love for her husband is not merely made up of sweet sentiments, honeyed phrases, or sentimental demonstrations: but it shows itself in active work, in practical enterprises, and in vital sacrifices for her husband. She takes a lively interest in his work or business, and assists him in either or both, directly or indirectly, according to her capacity. Above all she aims to render home to him what it should be to every good man: a haven of rest for the body and mind, a harbor of true happiness for the heart, and a genuine inspiration for the soul; a magnet to his entire being, from which he separates himself but with a pang, for which he longs with desire, and to which he returns with delight. To make such a paradise of her little home she spares neither thought nor study nor labor nor sacrifice. She feels happy and comfortable in knowing that she is contributing to the happiness and comfort of her husband. She loves, nourishes and cherishes her husband as her own body; and in loving him she loves herself and procures for herself the highest bliss this life contains.

The Disloyal Wife

In reviewing this ideal attitude of a Christian wife, many a woman may have to admit that in her life she fails to exhibit it. Perhaps her attachment to her husband is not so constant and whole-hearted as it should be. She has been disappointed in, or has grown tired of, married life. She begins to feel that she made a poor choice of a mate at best, and that she might have fared much better had she given herself more time to look about and select with care, or had she accepted the advances of this one or that one. The effect of such and similar thoughts and imaginations upon her marital fidelity is not good. She soon begins to weaken and long for other loves and new thrills of sexual alliances.

There may be conditions at home or elsewhere that nurse her temptations and fan her adulterous longings into real and effective desires. As the first woman, she gives ear to the insidious serpent, appearing to her in the way of a novel or magazine story, which she should have never read; or of a theatrical play or movie, which she should have never seen; or of a male friend or acquaintance, whom she should have never met; or of a boarder, roomer, laborer, salesman, or some professional man, whose first unbecoming approach or illicit advances she should have definitely and finally repulsed: the result is fatal and disastrous, to her virtue as well as to her peace, and often to her whole life's happiness and career. "The wages of sin is death." Resist the beginning, and you will never have to regret the end, of sin.

The Jealous Wife

There are other women who are perfectly and scrupulously loyal to their husbands, but who mar the easy and sweet tenor of married life by their abnormal suspiciousness and jealousy. Such a woman seems to take it for granted from the beginning of their marriage that her husband needs to be closely watched and carefully hedged about so as not to stray or deviate in his love. She lets him feel and know that she is not sure of him, and that it would not overly surprise, though it would terribly hurt her, if he struck out into forbidden byways of sexual adventures. She questions him at every turn, and demands a strict account of his every move, to render herself secure as to his marital constancy. She is quick in suspecting something wrong without any objective warrant, and she is just as hasty in accusing her husband openly and brutally of disloyalty, when not even the thought, desire, or hint of it ever entered his mind. It will be her fault and responsibility if in this case the innocent, ill-judged and falsely accused husband chafes and frets and revolts, and finally seeks redress by actuating the saying: "If I have the name, I may as well have the game."

The Lion and Dragon

In addition to being jealous and suspicious such a woman is usually given strongly to nagging. She likes to find fault with her husband, pick flaws in his conduct and manners, and criticize him for doing this and neglecting that. She derives pleasure from humiliating him, not only in private but also in public. Nor is she satisfied in blaming and vilifying him once or again for the same offense, but she repeats and rehashes it so often and so long as to render herself thoroughly obnoxious and extremely unsufferable. Of her the Bible says: "A wrangling wife is like a roof continually dropping through" (Prov. 19:13). "It is better to sit in a corner of the housetop, than with a brawling woman, and in a common house" (Prov. 21:9). "There is no anger above the anger of a woman. It will be more agreeable to abide with a lion and a dragon, than to dwell with a wicked woman" (Sir. 25:23). And if she kept her suspicions and complaints to herself, she might in the end be tolerable. Instead, eager to pose as a martyr, she retails them not only to her mother and other relatives but publishes them to the whole neighborhood to the poignant humiliation and disgrace of her husband.

They Expect Too Much

Moreover a jealous or suspicious woman has a morbid and inordinate craving for marks of affection and signs of endearment from her mate. She wants far more attention, consideration and coddling than a normal man, burdened with ordinary home and business interests, is capable of rendering. If he were to be as tireless in thinking of new ways and methods of pleasing, cajoling and surprising her with various demonstrations of love and adoration as she desires him to be, he would not only wear himself out, but also be unable to discharge other and more important duties. Yet if he does not meet her expectations, she charges him with being cold, indifferent, and disloyal.

Even otherwise good and sensible women are perhaps by their very sex, inclined to be rather exorbitant in their demands for, or expectations of love, affection, and recognition from their husbands. While they insist that the husbands should sympathetically understand and meet their needs and propensities, they fail to make a proportionate allowance for the nature and temperament of their husbands. If they did, they would comprehend that a man is often engrossed with serious business or other interests, and can therefore not occupy himself for the time being with the little amorous amenities and gallant pastimes of conjugal life. After all between the two, a good provider, though he be less of a gallant, is preferable to a charming gallant, who is a poor provider, as a husband.

The Foe of the Home

Mention must be made, too, of the idle, gallivanting, and frivolous wife, who seems to consider marriage as a title to empty enjoyment and carefree amusement. At home she feels ill at ease, and she is only happy when she has a date for a women's night out, a coffee, a movie or something similar. Her own house bores and tires her and makes her nervous. Consequently it gets the least of her attention and care. It is untidy, uninviting, and uncomfortable.[31] It is a

31 The same thing could be said about a spouse's appearance. Both a

sorry place for her husband to come to after his day's work, and a sadder place for him to live in when she constrains herself to keep him company. The meals are everything they should not be in the way of selection and preparation and service. The children, if there are any, are poorly cared for, they are unkempt and unclean, shabbily dressed, ill-trained and ill-mannered.

His home being the very opposite to what it ought to be, no wonder if the husband loathes it, and is eager to get away and stay away from it; and if he grows cold to and conceives a dislike for her who turns into a place of pain and agony, what to him should be nothing but a harbor of pleasure and repose.

To keep her home in order, to rear her children properly, to prepare good and tasty meals constitute a job so big that it requires practically all of a woman's time and attention to affect it squarely and satisfactorily. And if she so meets it, the very discharge of this arduous but sublime office as wife, mother, and homemaker will also represent the source of her most solid earthly happiness and her sweetest personal joys. These will be far superior to any thrill she could procure by always meandering about with other

---

husband and wife have a sacred obligation to care for their bodies—that is, to eat healthy and exercise. Although a mother will likely gain weight through the childbearing years, she must strive to keep her attractiveness for her husband and vice versa.

women to bars, theatres, shopping, and indulging in other parties at the expense of her sacred duties and solemn obligations. Everyone, also every married woman needs a certain amount of rest, recreation and diversion for her comfort and happiness; but excess in play is as bad or worse than excess in work.

Virtue and Common Sense

From all that has been said it is readily inferred that the marriage relation, perhaps more than any other in life, enjoins upon the parties to it the observance of the wise admonition of St. Paul, which I know I am repeating at the risk of becoming monotonous: "Bear ye one another's burdens." On the one hand there is no natural happiness greater and sweeter than that of married life: on the other the achievement of no other earthly happiness requires more virtue and good sense. Which of these two plays the bigger part in the pursuit of marital happiness it is hard to say. Perhaps the burden is equally divided. Yet for myself I am inclined to believe that good sense is in a way more operative in regard to happiness in married life and, for that matter, to the proper upbringing of children than is even virtue. This may strike some readers as surprising, to say the least, but it is nothing else than another rendering or another application of the well-known words of St. Teresa, who says that she preferred as her confessor a priest who was prudent but not holy to one who was holy but not prudent. More marriages are wrecked because of a lack of good common sense in one or both parties than because of a lack of virtue in both or in either. Certainly, the ideal condition is to have virtue and good sense joined in amicable proportions and in a good measure in both husband and wife.

She Was Contrary

In Rome they tell the story of a couple whose marriage was stormy and, consequently, most disagreeable throughout. To the wife it finally became so unbearable that she decided to put an end to her misery by plunging from a bridge into the swollen Tiber. Her husband, being apprised of the sad news, came to the river in search of the body. When the spot of her suicide was shown to him, he went up stream a considerable distance. They asked him why he went up stream, since the violent current had no doubt carried his wife's corpse far down stream. "You did not know my wife," he said archly, and not without sarcasm; "she was always contrary; and no doubt she kept the habit of it even after her death."

It is selfish stubbornness, as a rule, on the part of the husband or wife, or both, that wrecks many marriages which, by sensible concessions and compromises on both sides, could have been rendered exceedingly and permanently happy. But because the partners to them have not the good sense and virtue to make the necessary concessions, estrangements and ruptures soon ensue, and before long lead to an irremediable divorce.

Divorce

And since I mentioned the word "divorce," I may as well remind my readers once more that the marriage of Christians duly contracted, and consummated through cohabitation, can never be dissolved by any power on earth save by the death of one of the parties. Such a marriage can therefore never admit of an absolute divorce so one or both parties are free to marry during the lifetime of the respective partner. When the public press or the current gossip bring stories of divorced people being married in the Catholic Church, the first marriage for some publicly known or hidden reason was from the beginning null and void; or, the marriage was never consummated; or in case one of the parties was a non-baptized person, the so-called Pauline privilege[32] was invoked. At any rate, in all these cases

32 The Pauline privilege (1 Cor. 7:12–15) states that a marriage by two unbaptized persons can be dissolved when one of the spouses is baptized and seeks to enter a new marriage, provided the unbaptized person departs. See Can. 1143 for more details.

Catholic lay people will prudently withhold any adverse comments on the event, and leave the passing of judgment to the Church, being convinced the while, that a real divorce, in the above explained sense, has never been, and is never, and can never be, granted by the Church, according to the words of Christ: "What therefore God hath joined together, let no man put asunder" (Matt. 19:6).

Separation from Bed and Board

For very serious and urgent reasons the Church allows to married people what is called separation from bed and board. It even permits the innocent party, when necessary, for the same grave reasons, to apply to the civil court for separate maintenance or a civil divorce, to safeguard property and other rights, with the exclusion of the possibility of another marriage, of course, as long as the respective mate lives. Yet ordinarily such a separation and, much more, such an application to the civil courts must not be undertaken without the permission of the bishop, procured either directly, or through the pastor of the party in question.

Human nature being what it is, no two characters are so well balanced, and no two dispositions are so harmoniously poised, as to fit into each other in the proximity and intimacy of married life, as husband and wife, without considerable rectification and adjustment. And all those who contemplate marriage will do well in calculating on the necessity of a great deal of rearrangement in their own individual case after they are married, no matter to whom, and in being ready for it. This will forestall many a bitter disillusionment and many a keen regret, in addition to worse eventualities. Many, if not the majority of the disappointments in married life that seriously affect its happiness develop, not because the parties are what they are found to be after marriage, but because certain exaggerated and unwarranted expectations and appraisals of them had been formed and entertained by their mates before marriage.

The fault lay not in the realistic development after marriage, but in the extravagant illusions preceding it. A young man who is flattering himself that he is getting for his wife a faultless angel who will do nothing but remind him of paradise and heaven by her person and carriage; and the young lady who is sure she is marrying a perfect knight, whose one occupation after marriage will be to carry her on his hands and be at her bidding as a prince is to the fairy in the tale, are evidently too young, inexperienced and immature to launch out into the sea of matrimony, in which there are many and various treacherous cliffs to waylay and wreck their guileless and unsuspecting matrimonial craft.

Paint It Black

A Franciscan missionary bishop of China, returning to his native Religious province to recruit missionaries for his district, frankly, told the Franciscan clerics in submitting his case to them that if they had a desire to enlist for his mission, they should picture the conditions of a missionary in China as black and disagreeable as possible; and yet they could be sure that when they got there, they would find conditions even much worse than they had pictured them. Young people contemplating marriage might do well in following the same method. Of course, they would not invariably find marriage harder than they thus pictured it: but a little sobriety in the anticipations of married life will always make for more real contentment in the reality of it.

Caresses and Abuses

A young man came to a monastery and requested the superior to admit him as a member of the order. After looking him over carefully, the superior conducted him into the inner court of the cloister, led him up to a statue of a youth that was standing nearby, and bade him to praise, pet and fondle the statue for ten minutes and then to come and report to him in his office. When the young man reported, the superior asked him how the statue behaved. He replied that it showed no signs either of approval or disapproval. Then the superior bade the youth to take a whip which he handed him, and to lash the statue viciously for ten minutes, and again to report to him. When he returned, the superior asked him how the statue acted under the lashes, he answered that it behaved exactly as it did whilst it was being caressed. The superior rejoined: "If you can do the same in the convent; if you can suffer both praise and blame, reward and punishment with similar equanimity as the statue even though in a different, namely a rational manner, then you are a fit subject for the monastery: otherwise I should advise you not to enter." The point of this story is as applicable to candidates for marriage as it is to postulants for the Religious life.

Love Is Everything

Another inference we draw from all that has been said is the all-importance of love in married life. What the sun is in the physical life of the world, love is in the sphere of married life. Of it should be verified in every Christian marriage the words of the Apostle: "Charity (love) never falleth away: whether prophecies shall be made void, or tongues shall cease, or knowledge shall be destroyed" (1 Cor. 13:8). Youth will cease; beauty will fade; health will fail; friends will drop away; fame will vanish: just so love endures, strong, deep, devoted, and sweet between husband and wife, the disappearance of all else can easily be suffered: whereas if love dies away, no matter what else remains, married life is but a sad and pitiable specter of what it pretends and professes to be. "Love is strong as death" (Sg. 8:6).

Every Catholic home, whatever may be its financial status, or its material conditions and appointments, can be, and always is, one of three things: it is either a paradise, a purgatory, or a hell, depending upon the love that prevails or is lacking in it. Are you doing what you can to make a paradise of your home?

He Fell In the Creek

In conclusion I shall tell a story from the life of the great Catholic German parliamentarian Ludwig Windthorst. It is hardly an exaggeration to say that he did as much for the Catholic Church in Germany by fighting for and safeguarding its rights than any other layman, priest, bishop or cardinal. It was he particularly who successfully resisted and duly humiliated the powerful Bismarck, the Iron Chancellor. Windthorst was puny of stature and ungainly of figure; hence in his youth the girls were not especially interested in and fond of him. He had fallen in love with the charming daughter of a good Catholic family and, strong of will as he was, he was determined to win her for his wife, cost what it might. At first she gave him no encouragement. He persisted in his advances, however, hoping against hope that her heart would gradually soften towards him. One evening he was standing under the window of her room, which was in the second story in the rear of her home, and he serenaded her feelingly and intensely. Going backwards to look up and see if she was nodding approval, he forgot about the creek behind him, when he presently lost his footing and fell helpless into the water. As she saw him sprawling and splashing in the water, the young woman took pity on him. She came down from her room and asked him in the house to recover himself. While he was there they conversed, and before long the girl took quite a fancy to him and soon reciprocated his love fully, and in due time they were married.

Credit to Whom It is Due

When, after a half a century, they celebrated the golden jubilee of their marriage, all Catholic Germany gathered in its representatives to do honor to the Great Little Man who for many years was their captain and leader in the fierce struggle for their rights as citizens and Catholics. It was a grand demonstration of homage, recognition, reverence, and love. The aged warrior of Christ was visibly touched.

He was asked to make a speech. Even in his old age the marvelous and thrilling eloquence of his youth had not forsaken him. As he and his wife stood before the cheering and applauding audience, he motioned for silence and attention and said with much feeling and great earnestness: "My friends, you are not going to expect of me that I tell you how much I appreciate and how deeply I am impressed by the grand and whole-hearted exhibition of your love, gratitude and respect for me on this occasion. But I want to say and bring home to you this one thing: If in my life I have succeeded in doing something worthwhile for my God, my Church, and my country, I owe the achievement of it, after to God, to this noble woman at my side, whom God gave me as my helpmate. But for her encouragement, stimulation, and inspiration I should not be worthy of your plaudits and encomiums today. If you feel you must honor me, you must honor her as well, for she has made me what I am." The whole crowd broke into loud and endless applause at this fine and noble admission of the great man.

"So Say We All of Us"

I am satisfied that many of our Catholic men have made a success in life: not financially perhaps, or politically, or professionally: but, what counts infinitely more, morally, and religiously. They have been and are fine Catholic men, devoted husbands, good fathers, and loyal citizens. They have kept the faith and have handed it down to their children and their children's children, pure, staunch, and dynamic. Greater and more substantial success than this there is none in life. If these men were called upon to account for their success, most of them would have to give the credit of it to the noble women whom God gave to them as their helpmates. And no doubt the women in their turn would have to admit that their husbands helped them, too, to lead a better and purer life, to get closer to God and surer of heaven from day to day. This is what the Lord had in view when He made woman as a helpmate to man.

Mary and Joseph: The Ideal Couple

Besides exhibiting to Christian married couples, as an inspiring model of their mutual love, devotion and fidelity, His own union with His Church, our Lord also gives them another wondrous example in the marriage of His Blessed Mother and St. Joseph. They were poor and hard-working people. They had serious misfortunes and troubles, for instance: their failure to obtain suitable lodgings at the birth of Christ, their flight into Egypt, and the loss of the divine Child. But, thanks to their fear of the Lord and their mutual love, all their trials were easily borne, and tended rather to cement than slacken their sweet conjugal union.

There was a time, indeed, when Joseph, yet unacquainted with the mystery of the incarnation, "was minded to put her (Mary) away privately" (Matt. 1:19). But an angel of God warned him against it. What a terrible mistake would Joseph have made in jeopardy of his own best interests, had he separated from Mary! For one thing, he might never have died in the loving arms of Jesus and Mary. Even so Catholic married couples will ordinarily consult their welfare best if, instead of hastily deciding upon a rupture and a separation, when things of a mysterious or unpleasant nature develop, they man themselves to rise above all their difficulties and tribulations, with the help of their conjugal love, and their fear of and trust in the Lord. The sequel will as a rule distinctly justify and amply reward their self-control and wise sacrifice of personal inclinations and preferences.

All Aboard for God's Home and Ours

In the end I say once more, this life is a stage, on which you, as married Christian men, and women, as fathers and mothers, play a noble and difficult part. Soon the curtain will close on your play. If you are faithful to your part to the end—and with the grace of God this will not be hard—your death, in the language of one of the Holy Fathers, will not be a sad, but a glad day, a holy day, in fact. Your soul will be invited to its heavenly reward, while your body will be deposited in consecrated ground. The mound on your grave will long have sunk, and the inscription on your tombstone will have been rendered illegible through the years: but even then your memory will be held in benediction, and the germs of virtue which you spread about you will still be bearing fruit in your descendants, who in their time, when their little day is over, will follow you to their reward; and soon your earthly family will be housed, member for member, let us hope without a single exception, in the bright and happy home of God, Who is all love, and on Whose entrancing feast, prepared for His elect, the curtain will not close forevermore.

About the Author

Fr. Fulgence Meyer, OFM, was a noted retreat master and a prolific writer in the early twentieth century. He contributed to many Catholic papers and magazines. He published twenty-seven books and pamphlets—over a million copies of his books have been distributed. By June of 1951, over 420,000 copies of his book *Plain Talks* had been sold. He was born at Remich, Luxembourg on May 30, 1876. When he was nine, his family immigrated to the United States, and he entered St. Francis Preparatory Seminary in Cincinnati in 1888. Upon completion of his studies, he was received into the Franciscan Order in Mount Airy, Cincinnati, in 1892. He was ordained in Rome on July 15, 1900. A year later, he returned to the United States and was made lector of theology and humanities in the St. Clement Monastery House of Studies, St. Bernard. He was made rector of St. Francis Seraphic College, Cincinnati. From 1926 until his death, he lived at St. Francis Monastery, Cincinnati. He was a member of the board of directors for the Franciscan Province of St. John the Baptist in Cincinnati from 1930 to 1933. He died on November 14, 1938 in Mount Clemens, Michigan at the age sixty-two of pneumonia while conducting a mission in St. Lawrence Church, Utica, Michigan. A Requiem High Mass was held for him on November 17, 1938 at St. Francis Seraph Church, Cincinnati. He is buried at Saint Mary Cemetery, St. Bernard, Cincinnati.